FISHING THE ENGLISH LAKES

FISHING THE ENGLISH LAKES

Sidney Du Broff

Longman London and New York

Longman Group Limited
Longman House, Burnt Mill, Harlow
Essex CM20 2JE, England
Associated companies throughout the world

*Published in the United States of America
by Longman Inc., New York*

© Longman Group Limited 1983

All rights reserved. No part of this publication may be
reproduced, stored in a retrieval system, or transmitted
in any form or by any means, electronic, mechanical,
photocopying, recording, or otherwise, without the
prior permission of the Copyright owner.

First published 1983

British Library Cataloguing in Publication Data

Du Broff, Sidney
  Fishing the English lakes.
  1. Fishing–England
  I. Title
  639'.21'0942   SH257

  ISBN 0-582-50307-8

Library of Congress Cataloging in Publication Data

Du Broff, Sidney
  Fishing the English Lakes.
  1 Trout fishing–England
  2. Fishing–England
  3. Lakes–England
  I. Title
  SH688.G7D8 1983   799.1'755   82-12733

ISBN 0-582-50307-8 (pbk.)

Printed in Great Britain by
Pitman Press Ltd., Bath

DEDICATION

This book is dedicated to my wife Nedra for all her help and to all of those who create the lakes and who maintain them.

CONTENTS

Introduction	ix
Alphabetical list of lakes	1
The Water Authorities	171
The lakes listed by county	172
Conversion tables	175

INTRODUCTION

The English lakes, created of necessity, are man's gift to Nature and to himself. All who fish for trout with a fly are indebted to those creators, who have made our lives better and the country richer. The fact that Nature has largely overlooked us has not kept us from casting our flies on the sparkling lakes that dot almost every area of this fisherman's happy land. Ironically, the waters that Mother Nature did create are not regarded as serious venues by most trout fishermen.

The lakes included here are in alphabetical order. If you intend to visit a particular area and would like to know what lakes are included in it, turn to the back of the book where there is a County listing.

Waters not listed here are those that did not wish to be included, since they have as many visitors as their facilities can accommodate. Prices, since they have a tendency to rise, are given by range, only as an approximation.

It is hoped that this Guide will serve your fishing needs well, and open up new fishing horizons that will contribute handsomely to your bag.

My thanks to all who have contributed so generously of their time and effort in providing the data here included, and to the general editor, Diane Burston, for all her ideas, suggestions, help and patience.

The data which has been supplied is correct in so far as it is known. The reader is asked to bear in mind that situations and circumstances alter, and that what may appear to be inaccuracies are due to changes for which we cannot account.

Sidney Du Broff

ALPHABETICAL LIST OF LAKES

ALLENS FARM
Rockbourne Road, Sandleheath, near Fordingbridge, Hants
Tel: Rockbourne (072 53) 313

Location: Off B3078, near A338. Near Fordingbridge between Ringwood and Salisbury

THE WATER:	Five lakes totalling approximately 8 acres. 2 to 3 miles of chalk stream. Fishing hut with WC. Flies, leaders, fair range of tackle available from office. Maximum number of rods per day: 23.
SEASON:	Mid-March to end of October.
HOURS:	8.30 a.m. until half-hour after sunset.

		Price band (£)
COSTS:	Full rod (1 named day per week, 4 fish per day)	250.00–280.00
	Half rod (1 named day per fortnight, 4 fish per day)	125.00–140.00
	Day ticket (4 fish)	9.00–10.50
	Half-day ticket (to or from 2.00 p.m.) (3 fish)	7.25–8.50
	Evening ticket (2 fish)	5.50–6.50

All prices include VAT
Additional tickets available.

STOCKING POLICY:	Stocking is carried out on a direct replacement basis (at least five times per week) plus 10% per week for losses. Size range: $1\frac{1}{4}$ lb to 10–12 lb. Average: $1\frac{3}{4}$ lb.
PERMITS:	Reservations not required, but recommended. Wessex Water Authority rod licence required, available on premises.
GENERAL INFORMATION:	7,096 fish taken by 2,885 rods (an average of 2.46 fish per rod visit)

The water is clear and extremely fertile. Imitative patterns almost always do very much better than traditional/attractor patterns or lures. Because the water is extremely clear, stealth and concealment are also pre-requisites to success.

NAC Grade I coaching is available by prior arrangement.

ARDINGLY RESERVOIR
Haywards Heath, West Sussex
Tel: Haywards Heath (0444) 892549

Location: Off B2028 Haywards Heath to Turners Hill Road

THE WATER:	180 acres. Lodge. WC.	
SEASON:	Mid-April to end October.	
HOURS:	Sunrise to one hour after sunset.	
		Price band (£)
COSTS:	Day ticket (weekdays, 6 fish)	4.50–5.50
	Day ticket (weekends, 6 fish)	5.00–6.00
BOATS:	Single and double boats available Costs: Single: £4.00–5.00 per day Double: £5.50–6.50 per day	
STOCKING POLICY:	Stocking as required.	
PERMITS:	Reservations recommended. Southern Water Authority licence required.	
GENERAL INFORMATION:	Depth at dam – 40 ft +. Mixed rainbows and browns. Fish generally in the $1\frac{1}{4}$ lb range. Large area of bank closed to fishing.	

ARDLEIGH RESERVOIR
Clover Way, near Colchester, Essex
Tel: Colchester (0206) 230642

Location: Off A137 Colchester Road

THE WATER:	130 acres. Shelter. WCs.	
SEASON:	1 April to 30 September.	
HOURS:	8.00 a.m. to one hour after sunset.	
		Price band (£)
COSTS:	Full rod (all days during season)	155.00–185.00
	Full rod (weekdays only)	115.00–140.00
	Day ticket (6 fish)	6.00–7.00
	Evening ticket	3.70–4.25
	Juniors (18 years and under)	1.80–2.25
	All prices include VAT	
BOATS:	Costs: £7.00–8.00 per day	
	£4.50–5.50 per evening	
STOCKING POLICY:	Well-stocked with rainbows and browns in the 1 lb range.	
PERMITS:	Reservations recommended. Anglian Water Authority licence required.	
GENERAL INFORMATION:	Angling instruction can be arranged.	

ARGAL RESERVOIR
Penryn, near Falmouth, Cornwall
Tel: Penryn (0326) 72544

Location: Off B3291 near Penryn

THE WATER:	65 acres. No lodge facilities. No limit to number of rods.	
SEASON:	1 April to 31 October.	
HOURS:	One hour before sunrise to one hour after sunset.	
COSTS:		*Price band (£)*
	Day ticket (5 fish)	4.50–6.00
	OAP, disabled, student under 18, junior under 16	3.50–5.00
	Child under 14	1.00–1.50
	Evening ticket (after 4.00 p.m., 3 fish)	2.50–3.50

Book of 20 permits available at 15% discount.
No additional day tickets available.

BOATS: Pulling boats available, seats 2. Anchors provided. No boats Thursday or Fridays. No boats after 12 October.
Costs: £4.50–5.50 per day
    £3.00–3.50 half day (after 4.00 p.m.)
Telephone Warden to book.

STOCKING POLICY: Pre-season stocking of browns and rainbows, then trickle stocking throughout season with fish averaging over 1 lb.

PERMITS: No reservations required. Tickets on self-service, no change available. No water authority licence required.

GENERAL INFORMATION: 4,642 fish caught during season. 1.8 fish per rod day.
Lures in April, but their effectiveness dwindles during the season. Late May normally sees the start of the Hawthorn hatch when imitations can produce hectic sport. During the summer fish feed heavily on damsel nymphs, particularly green patterns. Orange flies work well during daphnia blooms of summer. Late season, Invicta and Daddy Longlegs prove successful. Small black flies are a good stand-by throughout the season. Sheltered as this water is, rising fish can normally be found and surface fishing can be enjoyed on most days.

South West Water Authority

ASHMERE FISHERIES
Felix Lane, Shepperton, Middlesex
No telephone

Location: Off B375, near junction with A244

THE WATER:	Season only. Two lakes of 4 acres and 15 acres. Lodge facilities available.
SEASON:	1 March to 15 July and 15 September to 15 November.
HOURS:	No set time.
COSTS:	Prices only available by post to individual enquirers (varies with type of membership). Young people free if a parent is a member.
BOATS:	Boats available.
STOCKING POLICY:	Rainbows only. Stocking every 10 days.
PERMITS:	Thames Water Authority licence required, available on premises.

AVINGTON TROUT FISHERY LIMITED
Itchen Abbas, Winchester, Hampshire
Tel: Itchen Abbas (096278) 312

Location: Near Avington, near Itchen Abbas. Near B3047/A31. Off A33 Winchester by-pass

THE WATER:	Three lakes totalling 13 acres. WC. Maximum number of rods per day: 35.	
SEASON:	Beginning April to end October.	
HOURS:	9.00 a.m. to sunset.	
COSTS	Day ticket (4 fish)	*Price band (£)* 12.85–14.50
	Juniors (half-price, 2 fish) Additional day tickets available, same price as above.	
STOCKING POLICY:	Stocked only to replace fish taken.	
PERMITS:	Reservations required. No water authority licence required.	
GENERAL INFORMATION:	Single flies only, 1 in. maximum. Green nymphs, fished deep, sometimes do well.	

BAGWELL GREEN

Greenways Farm, Winchfield, near Basingstoke, Hants
No telephone

Location: Off A3016 — from M3 at Odiham or A30 Phoenix Green, Hartley Wintney

THE WATER:	Two lakes of ¾ acre and 1 acre. Flies available.	
SEASON:	Beginning April to end October.	
HOURS:	9.30 a.m. to sunset.	
		Price band (£)
COSTS:	Full rod	60.00–75.00
	Day ticket (2 fish)	4.00–5.00
STOCKING POLICY:	Stocking takes place early in the season.	
PERMITS:	Reservations required.	

BAKETHIN RESERVOIR
Northumberland
Tel: Kielder (0660) 50260 (9.30 a.m. to 10.30 a.m.)
c/o Northumbrian Water Authority, Northumberland and Tyne Division,
Northumbria House, Town Centre, Cramlington

Location: Road to Butteryhaugh. Signposted from North Tyne (C200) road. Near Kielder village. Near B632

THE WATER:	138 acres. Altitude 600 ft. Lodge facilities. WC. Other facilities in area. Maximum number of rods per day: 50.	
SEASON:	1 April to 30 September.	
HOURS:	6.00 a.m. to 7.00 p.m.	
		Price band (£)
COSTS:	Full rod (8 fish, 9 in. minimum size)	100.00 +
	OAP, disabled and children under 16	50.00 +
	Day ticket (8 fish, 9 in. minimum size)	4.00 +
	OAP, disabled and children under 16	2.00 +
	Weekly ticket	16.00 +
	OAP, disabled and children under 16	8.00 +
BOATS:	Five rowing boats available, seats 2, from 8.30 a.m. May be reserved. Costs: £5.00 + per day £3.00 + per evening.	
STOCKING POLICY:	Brown trout only.	
PERMITS:	50 permits issued daily. No reservations required. Self-service facilities for day tickets. Northumbrian Water Authority licence required, contact Northumberland and Tyne Division (address above).	
GENERAL INFORMATION:	Worm or fly. 3,184 fish taken by 1,352 (recorded) rods. Camping, caravan sites and accommodation nearby.	

BALDERHEAD RESERVOIR
Co. Durham
c/o Northumbrian Water Authority, Tees Division, Trenchard Avenue,
Thornaby, Stockton, Cleveland
Tel: Stockton (0642) 62216

*Location: Approached from Romaldkirk, through Hunderthwaite village.
Near Barnard Castle*

THE WATER:	576 acres. Altitude 1090 ft. Lodge facilities. WC. Maximum number of rods per day: 10.	
SEASON:	22 March to 30 September.	
HOURS:	6.00 a.m. to 7.00 p.m.	
		Price band (£)
COSTS:	Day ticket (8 fish, 9 in. minimum size)	2.00 +
	OAP, disabled, children under 16	1.00 +
PERMITS:	No reservations. But only 10 places available. Water is club-controlled. Self-service facilities for day tickets. Northumbrian Water Authority licence required, contact Tees Division (address above).	
GENERAL INFORMATION:	Browns only. Unstocked. Fly or worm. 477 fish taken by 373 (recorded) rods	

BANK HOUSE FLY FISHERY
Low Mill, Lancaster Road, Caton, near Lancaster, Lancs
Tel: Caton (0524) 770412

Location: Near A683, near M6, Junction 34

THE WATER:	2 acres. Lodge facilities including lounge, kitchen with cooking facilities, utensils, cutlery and linen. WC. Maximum number of rods per day: 6.
SEASON:	1 March to 31 October.
HOURS:	9.00 a.m. until one hour after dusk.

COSTS:

	Price band (£)
Full rod (day to be specified/4 fish)	330.00–370.00
Day tickets (4 fish)	11.00–12.00
Half-day tickets (2 fish)	7.00–8.00
Evening tickets (2 fish)	7.00–8.00

Fishermen are allowed to carry on fishing after having caught their limit, but if intend to kill further brace, must first pay £4.00 extra. Otherwise all further fish must carefully be returned to water. Catches may be inspected at random.

STOCKING POLICY:	Stocked daily. Average weight of fish 2 lb, about 75 fish per acre. Weight range: 1 lb to 10 lb. 3 rainbows to 1 brown and 1 brook.
PERMITS:	Reservations required.
GENERAL INFORMATION:	2,750 fish taken by 880 day rods. Nymph fishing recommended early on, wet and dry fly from May onwards. Fish well dispersed. Browns nearer to inflow. No long shank hooks. Size No. 10 maximum. No muddlers, baby dolls, streamers.

BARN ELMS RESERVOIRS
Merthyr Terrace, off Castelnau, Hammersmith, London
Tel: 01-748 3423

Location: Near A4, Hammersmith Broadway, London. Off A306. Near Barnes Railway Station and Hammersmith Broadway Underground station

THE WATER:	Three reservoirs, each approximately 20 acres. Lodge facilities. WC. Maximum number of rods per day: Boat reservoir: normally 24–28; any method reservoir (bank): 90; fly only reservoir (bank): 60.
SEASON:	Mid-March to end November.
HOURS:	7.30 a.m. or sunrise (whichever is later) to half-hour after sunset.

COSTS:

	Price band (£)
Day ticket (weekdays, 6 fish)	5.60–6.25
Day ticket (weekends/Bank holidays, 6 fish)	7.20–8.00
Half-day ticket (weekdays, 4 fish)	4.00–4.50
Half-day ticket (weekends/Bank holidays, 4 fish)	5.60–6.25

All prices include VAT

Half price for under-16s except for first month of season when full price is charged.
Additional day tickets available, same price as above.

BOATS: Row boats for one or two anglers on one reservoir.
Approximately 12–14 boats available.
Costs: £3.30–3.75 per day; £2.50–2.80 half day
    Weekends/Bank holidays: £4.40–5.00 per day;
    £3.30–3.75 half day.

STOCKING POLICY: About 80 fish per acre on the fly-only reservoir; 70 fish per acre on the any-method reservoir, and 40 fish per acre on boat fishery. Daily stocking. Numbers stocked depend on how well it is fishing. Aim to give catch rate for the season of 1.5–2.0 fish per permit. No fish under 12 in. stocked. Nearly all rainbows, small number of browns.

PERMITS: Reservations advised for first week of season. Thames Water Authority rod licence required (available at reservoir).

GENERAL INFORMATION: 32,369 fish taken by 18,757 rods.
Reservoirs are square and approximately 15 to 20 ft deep. Banks are steep sloping.
    Early and late in the season, light or dark lures on a sinking line, fished deep and slow. The occasional warm and sunny day could see hatch of chironemids, when a

floating line will do well. Nymphs, often green ones, will do well during the rest of the season, with the sedges coming on in summer. On hot, bright, still days the fish switch off, either because they have fed their fill or because water temperatures are high and oxygen content correspondingly low. Fish move to the middle of the water and go deep into the coolest part of the lake. Also, during the period when the fine, brown algae blossoms, the fish go into a sulk; with feeding, when it does occur, taking place during the last 15 or 30 minutes of the day.

Thames Water Authority Reservoir

BARROWS RESERVOIRS
c/o Bristol Waterworks, Woodford Lodge, Chew Stoke, Bristol
Tel: Chew Magna (027 589) 2339

Location: Off A38 about 5 miles south of Bristol

THE WATER:	Three lakes, 26, 39 and 60 acres. No limit to number of rods. WC. Shelters.
SEASON:	Early April to 15 October.
HOURS:	One hour before sunrise to one hour after sunset.

		Price band (£)
COSTS:	Full rod (covering Blagdon, Chew Valley Lake and the Barrows, 8 fish per day)	200.00–250.00
	Full rod (husband and wife) as above	350.00–425.00
	Full rod (Barrows only, 8 fish per day)	90.00–110.00
	Full rod (OAP, disabled) Barrows only, Monday to Friday	45.00–60.00
	Full rod (Juniors and full-time students) Barrows only	35.00–45.00
	Day ticket (Barrows only, 8 fish)	4.00–5.00
	Day ticket (OAP, disabled, juniors) Barrows only	2.00–3.00

Prices inclusive of VAT and Wessex Water Authority licence fees.

STOCKING POLICY:	Spring stocking followed by staggered restocking during season. All Bristol trout lakes: 100,000 brown and rainbow trout. Size 1 lb+ to 2 lb+. 50% browns, 50% rainbows.
PERMITS:	Reservations not required. Self-service kiosk for bank permits. No local waterboard licence required.
GENERAL INFORMATION:	5,785 fish caught during season. Average weight: 1 lb. Best brown: 6.08 lb, best rainbow: 6.15 lb. Full rods are eligible for £1.00 reduction on the cost of any day permit at Chew Valley Lake or Blagdon (bank or boat). Start season: Lures, sunk lines Late May/June: Smaller flies, floating lines Summer: Floating lines, nymphs and small flies September: Floating lines, smaller flies Late season: Sunk lines and lures Accommodation is available in the area. Contact Bristol Waterworks for list.

BAYHAM LAKE TROUT FISHERY LIMITED
Bayham Abbey, Lamberhurst, Tunbridge Wells, Kent
Tel: Lamberhurst (0892) 890276

Location: Near Lamberhurst, near Tunbridge Wells. Off B2169, near A21, near A267, near B2100

THE WATER:	16 acres. Fishing lodge. Refreshments. Tackle shop. Seats, rest huts and storm shelters around fishery. Maximum number of rods per day: 35 (including boats).	
SEASON:	Beginning April to end October.	
HOURS:	Day and half-day rods from 7.30 a.m. until one hour after sunset. Season rods start at sunrise.	

COSTS:

Price band (£)

	Normal*	Alternative†
Day ticket	9.00–10.50	15.00 (4 fish)–17.00
Half-day ticket	6.00–7.00	9.00 (2 fish)–10.50
Full rod (28×1 day)	232.00–260.00	390.00 (4 fish)–450.00
Half rod (14×1 day)	117.00–135.00	195.00 (4 fish)–225.00

All prices include VAT
* Plus cost of fish by the pound (Approximately £1.00 per lb)
† To include the fish without additional cost

Absolute limit of eight fish per session, applicable to all rods. Rods may retain or return fish at their discretion. Concessions for beginners of all ages.
One additional day ticket available, same price as above.

BOATS:	Five boats available. Maximum 2 rods per boat. Reservations recommended. Anchors provided (2 per boat). Costs: Single, £5.00–6.00 per day; £3.50–4.25 half day Double, £7.00–8.25 per day; £5.00–6.00 half day
STOCKING POLICY:	$1\frac{1}{2}$ lb to 12 lb (average $2\frac{1}{2}$ lb). 100 fish per acre, restocked weekly, to replace previous week's catch.
PERMITS:	Reservations recommended. Southern Water Authority licence required (available from Lodge).
GENERAL INFORMATION:	9,737 fish taken by 3,044 rods. The lake is relatively shallow, ranging from 9 ft to 4 ft 6 in. It is best fished with floating line. The Cascade Pools, below the outfall of the River Teise fish consistently well throughout the season and are

particularly productive when fished with a leaded shrimp cast into the white water beneath each waterfall.

5 lb breaking strain leader recommended. Single hook No. 8 maximum. Fishing from a boat, anchored: east of Osprey Island; off the dam, along a line parallel with boat jetty; close to rhododendrons along north bank.

BELLBROOK VALLEY TROUT FISHERY
Bellbrook, Oakford, near Tiverton, Devon
Tel: Oakford (039 85) 292

Location: Approximately 6 miles west of Tiverton, off B3221 or can be approached off A361 Barnstaple Road. Oakford village clearly signed on left of road, 1 mile from Black Cat crossroads

THE WATER:	4 acres. Rods may be hired. Flies available. WCs. Maximum number of rods per day: 16.
SEASON:	Mid-March to Christmas.
HOURS:	First light to last light.

		Price band (£)
COSTS:	Day ticket (8 fish)	5.00–6.50
	Half-day ticket (4 fish)	2.50–3.50

(Note: All fish to be paid for at £1.00 per lb.)
Any number of half-day tickets to be held in one day.

STOCKING POLICY:	About 500 fish per acre. Pre-stock as required, about every two weeks during season. 1 lb to 7–8 lb. Rainbows.
PERMITS:	Reservations advisable. Self-booking-in system. No water authority licence required.
GENERAL INFORMATION:	3.4 fish per rod average. Water is from 5 ft to 16 ft. Local pub for accommodation and food in Oakford village.

BEWL BRIDGE RESERVOIR
Bewl Bridge Lane, Lamberhurst, Tunbridge Wells, Kent
Tel: Lamberhurst (0892) 890352

Location: 1 mile south of Lamberhurst village on A21 (London–Hastings road)

THE WATER:	770 acres. Lodge facilities. Permits, tackle, flies. WC close by. No limit to number of rods (except for first day).	
SEASON:	7 April to 17 October.	
HOURS:	Sunrise to one hour after sunset.	
COSTS:		*Price band (£)*
	Full rod (6 fish per day)	190.00–225.00
	Weekday full rod (Monday–Friday)	145.00–180.00
	Weekly permit	40.00–55.00
	Junior full rod	140.00–175.00
	Junior one month	40.00–55.00
	Day ticket (weekday, 6 fish)	5.50–7.00
	Day ticket (weekend & holidays, 6 fish)	6.50–8.00
	Junior day ticket	4.50–5.50
	Evening ticket (weekday)	4.50–5.50
	Evening ticket (weekend & holidays)	5.00–6.25

Additional day tickets available, same price as above.

BOATS:	29 motor boats. 18 rowing boats. To accommodate 1 to 3 anglers. Anchors provided. Reservations recommended. Costs: Motor boat: single, £7.50–9.00 per day Motor boat: double, £10.00–12.00 per day Rowing boat: single, £4.00–5.00 per day Rowing boat: double, £5.50–6.50 per day Evening hire also available.
STOCKING POLICY:	Stocking with rainbows, browns and occasionally brooks. Approximately 70 fish per acre. Stocking weekly but more frequently, if required. Minimum 12 in. Usually between 1 lb to 2 lb.
PERMITS:	No reservations required (other than opening day). Self-service arrangements available for bank fishermen when fishing lodge is closed. Water authority licence not required for day ticket anglers.
GENERAL INFORMATION:	44,591 fish taken by 19,057 rods. Southern Water Authority.

BICKTON MILL LAKES
Bickton, Fordingbridge, Hants
Tel: Fordingbridge (0425) 52236

Location: Off A338, near Fordingbridge

THE WATER:	Two small lakes. Maximum number of rods per day: 8.	
SEASON:	Beginning April to mid-October.	
HOURS:	9.00 a.m. to 9.00 p.m.	
		Price band (£)
COSTS:	Day ticket (3 fish)	6.00–7.50
PERMITS:	Reservations required.	
GENERAL INFORMATION:	Dry fly or nymph.	

BLACKTON RESERVOIR
Co Durham
c/o Northumbrian Water Authority, Tees Division, Trenchard Avenue,
Thornaby, Stockton, Cleveland
Tel: Stockton (0642) 62216

Location: Via Cotherstone. Near Barnard Castle

THE WATER:	110 acres. Lodge facilities. WC. Maximum number of rods per day: 10.	
SEASON:	22 March to 30 September.	
HOURS:	6.00 a.m. to 7.00 p.m.	
		Price band (£)
COSTS:	Day ticket (8 fish, 9 in. minimum size)	2.00 +
	OAP, disabled, children under 16	1.00 +
PERMITS:	No reservations required. But only 10 places available. Water is club-controlled. Self-service facilities for day tickets. Northumbrian Water Authority licence required, contact Tees Division (address above).	
GENERAL INFORMATION:	Browns only. Unstocked. Fly or worm. 291 fish taken by 62 (recorded) rods.	

BLAGDON LAKE
c/o Bristol Waterworks, Woodford Lodge, Chew Stoke, Bristol
Tel: Chew Magna (027 589) 2339

Location: 14 miles south of Bristol. Off A368 near junction with A38

THE WATER:	440 acres. Lodge facilities including WC, drying room, tackle shop. No limit to number of rods.
SEASON:	Early April to 15 October.
HOURS:	One hour before sunrise to one hour after sunset. Boat fishing from 10.00 a.m. to one hour after sunset.

Price band (£)

COSTS:	Full rod (covering Blagdon, Chew Valley Lake and the Barrows, 8 fish per day)	200.00–250.00
	Full rod (Husband and Wife) as above	350–425.00
	Full rod (OAP, disabled) Monday to Friday	110.00–150.00
	Full rod (Juniors and full-time students)	85.00–110.00
	Day ticket (8 fish)	5.00–7.00
	Day ticket (OAP, disabled, juniors)	2.50–4.00

Prices inclusive of VAT and Wessex Water Authority licence fees.

BOATS:	Rowing boats available. Maximum 3 fishermen per boat. Juniors must be accompanied by adult. Minimum fee for one rod in boat.
	Costs: £10.50–12.50 per day.
	  £7.50–9.50 per day (OAP, disabled and junior)
	  Minimum fee for one rod using boat: £12.00–14.00.

STOCKING POLICY:	Spring stocking followed by staggered restocking during season. All Bristol trout lakes: 100,000 brown and rainbow trout. Size 1 lb+ to 2 lb+. 50% browns, 50% rainbows.
PERMITS:	Reservations required for boat fishing only. Self-service kiosk for bank permits. No local waterboard licence required.

GENERAL INFORMATION:	16,949 fish caught during season. Average weight: 1.15 lb. Best brown: 6.05 lb. Best rainbow: 11 lb. 185 fish in 4 lb to 5 lb range. 11 fish in 5 lb to 6 lb range. 15 fish over 6 lb.
	  Full rods are eligible for £3.00 reduction on cost of day boat and £1.50 after 3.00 p.m.
	Start season: Lures, sunk lines.
	Late May/June: Smaller flies, floating lines.
	Summer: Floating lines, nymphs and small flies.
	September: Floating lines, smaller flies.
	Late season: Sunk lines and lures.
	  Accommodation is available in the area. Contact Bristol Waterworks for list.

BLOCK FEN DROVE
Chatteris, Cambridgeshire
Tel: Chatteris (03543) 3214 (10.30 a.m.–11.30 a.m. and 12.30 p.m.–4.30 p.m.)
Further inquiries: Chatteris Aqua Sports Ltd, Strafford House, Wentworth, Cambs. Tel: Ely (0353) 778332 (after 6.30 p.m.)

Location: Turn off A142 Ely to Chatteris via Mepal

THE WATER:	70 acres.
SEASON:	1 April to end October.
HOURS:	7.00 a.m. to one hour after sunset.
COSTS:	Prices only available to individual enquirers.
BOATS:	Boats available.
PERMITS:	Reservations recommended.
GENERAL INFORMATION:	About 1.5 fish per rod.

BRIDGE FARM TROUT LAKES
65, The Street, Old Basing, Basingstoke, Hampshire.
Tel: Basingstoke (0256) 65939

Location: 2 miles east of Basingstoke in the middle of Old Basing next to the railway line. The lakes are at the rear of Bridge Farm Shop

THE WATER:	Lakes totalling approximately 3 acres. Fishing hut with seats. WC. Flies available. Maximum number of rods per day: 12.
SEASON:	1 April to 31 October.
HOURS:	8.00 a.m. to 9.00 p.m. or sunset, whichever is sooner.
COSTS:	*Price band (£)* Day ticket (4 fish) 10.00–11.00 + VAT Evening ticket when available (2 fish) 5.00–6.00 + VAT Additional day ticket/evening ticket available, same price as above.
STOCKING POLICY:	Daily put-and-take basis. Stock consists of approx 65% rainbows (1 lb to 9 lb) and 35% browns (1 lb to 5 lb). Approximately 100 fish per acre. River section holds a stock of wild browns and is stocked with a small amount of rainbows 14 oz to 2½ lb.
PERMITS:	Reservations advisable, preferable before 9 p.m. Thames Water Authority licence required, not available on premises.

GENERAL INFORMATION:	591 fish taken by 276 rods, including 204 evening. Overall average: 1 lb 13½ oz. Average bag per day: 3.39 fish. Biggest rainbow: 8 lb 4 oz. Biggest brown: 6 lb 12 oz.
	    All parts of the lakes can be successfully fished with a floating line; a long leader is useful. During April most fish are caught below the surface. Popular patterns are Pheasant Tails, shrimp imitations (leaded for deep areas), and Black and Peacock Spiders fished slowly near the surface on warm days.
	    Late spring (warm days produce good rises): use dry fly, buzzers, tiny midge imitations.
	    Summer: fair hatches of sedges, particularly around areas of fast water. Fishing still on surface, sedge pupa imitations fished at various depths, retrieved at a steady pace.
	    Autumn: large nymph useful when fish hunting for fly and beetles.
	    Good sport near the over-hanging trees, as insects are blown onto the water, especially by the side streams.
	    Fish in the river feed mainly on olives and nymphs, shrimps at the beginning of the season, later on mayfly and sedge, mostly on the surface.

BRIDLINGTON TROUT FISHERY
Hempholme Road, Brandesburton, Humberside
Tel: Leven (0401) 43631

Location: Take Hempholme Road out of Brandesburton and follow White Rabbit signs

THE WATER:	10 acres. Some tackle available. Maximum number of rods per day: 40–50. Snack caravan for use as a shelter. WC.	
SEASON:	Open all year.	
HOURS:	Summer: 9.00 a.m. to 9.00 p.m. Winter: 9.00 a.m. to 5.00 p.m.	
COSTS:	Day ticket (9.00 a.m. to 9.00 p.m., 2 fish) Day ticket (9.00 a.m. to 5.00 p.m., 2 fish) Any 4 hours (1 fish) £1.00 reduction for young people.	*Price band (£)* 7.00–8.50 6.00–7.50 3.00–4.00
	Additional tickets available, £6.00–7.50 per day, £3.00–4.00 per 4 hour session.	
BOATS:	Four boats available. 1–2 fishermen per boat. Reservations recommended. Anchors provided. Costs: £5.00–6.00 per day. £3.00–4.00 per 4-hour session.	
STOCKING POLICY:	Stocking every 3 to 4 weeks, 200 fish at a time. 200 fish per acre. 90% rainbows, 10% brooks. $1\frac{1}{4}$ lb to 10 lb.	
PERMITS:	Reservations advisable, but not required. Yorkshire Water Authority licence required, not available at lake.	

GENERAL INFORMATION:	461 fish taken by 153 anglers during 15 day period: 1 to 15 October. Largest fish 5 lb 4 oz.
	  The depth of the water varies from 20 ft to 45 ft, fishable from 75% of the bank.
	  When two-fish limit has been reached, you can continue fishing, with a barbless hook, returning all fish caught.
	  Local fish shop supplies dinners Wednesday, Friday and Saturday lunchtimes and some evenings. Bed and breakfast offered in Bridlington.	

BROADFIELD TROUT LAKE
Broadfield Farm, Great Somerford, near Chippenham, Wilts.
Tel: Seagry (0249) 720292

*Location: M4 Junction 17. Great Somerford 3½ miles. Fishery in the village.
Nearest towns: Chippenham 6 miles; Malmesbury 4 miles; Swindon 15 miles*

THE WATER:	5 acres. Fishing hut. WC. Maximum number of rods per day: 4.
SEASON:	Mid-April to mid-October.
HOURS:	9.00 a.m. to 9.00 p.m. or dusk.
COSTS:	Information regarding cost and bag limit not available. No additional day tickets available.
STOCKING POLICY:	50 to 70 fish per acre. 67% rainbow trout, 33% brown trout. 1 lb to 1½ lb average but larger fish present.
PERMITS:	Reservations required. No water authority licence required.
GENERAL INFORMATION:	Lake depth 13 ft maximum. Floating lines only. Maximum size fly No. 10 long shank. One fly on leader.

BUCKMINSTER PARK LAKE
Buckminster, Nr. Grantham, Lincolnshire
Tel: Grantham (0476) 860471

Location: Off the Buckminster-Sproxton Road

THE WATER:	Approximately 7 acres. Timber hut, interior seating, washing and weighing facilities. Elsan facilities at rear. Pub in village, 1 mile. Maximum number of rods per day: 18.	
SEASON:	1 April to 31 September.	
HOURS:	Dawn to dusk.	
		Price band (£)
COSTS:	Full rod (1 day per week – Monday to Thursday, 4 fish per day)	140.00–170.00
	Half rod (as above)	70.00–85.00
	Full rod (1 day per week – Friday to Sunday, 4 fish per day)	180.00–210.00
	Half rod (as above)	90.00–105.00
	Day tickets (Monday to Thursday, 4 fish)	7.00–8.30
	Day tickets (Friday to Sunday, 4 fish)	9.00–11.00
	Evening tickets (from 5.00 p.m., 2 fish)	5.00–6.00
	Additional day tickets available.	
STOCKING POLICY:	100 to 120 fish per acre. Stocking in October, then three or four times during season. Normal input: 300 to 500 rainbows and browns, averaging 1 lb+. Two rainbows to one brown.	
PERMITS:	Reservations recommended. Anglian Water Authority licence required, not available on premises.	
GENERAL INFORMATION:	600 fish taken by 155 rods (Season ticket-holders each counting as one rod). Deepest water in bay from immediate frontage of fishing hut round to right towards dam some 15 ft. Between island and dam some 6 ft to 8 ft. Island to inlet shallows off, but with deeper gullies cut during construction. Single fly only. No dogs allowed.	

BULL MEADOW LAKE
Portmore Farm, Jordan's Lane, Boldre, Lymington, Hants
Tel: Lymington (0590) 73810

Location: Off A337, near Lymington

THE WATER:	1 acre.	
SEASON:	Beginning April to end October.	
HOURS:	9.00 a.m. to sunset.	
		Price band (£)
COSTS:	Day ticket (5 fish)	8.25–10.00
	Half-day tickets (3 fish)	5.00–6.75
	Evening ticket (2 fish)	3.50–5.00
PERMITS:	Reservations recommended.	
GENERAL INFORMATION:	No lures.	

BUREBANK TROUT FISHERY
Itteringham, near Aylsham, Norfolk
Tel: Saxthorpe (026 387) 666

Location: Off B1354 near B1149. Near Aylsham

THE WATER:	3 to 4 acres plus stream.	
SEASON:	Beginning April to end October.	
HOURS:	8.30 a.m. to dusk.	
		Price band (£)
COSTS:	Day ticket (4 fish)	5.50–7.00
	Evening ticket (2 fish)	4.50–5.75

BURNHOPE RESERVOIR

Co. Durham
c/o Northumbrian Water Authority, Wear Division, Wear House, Abbey Road, Pity Me, Durham
Tel: Durham (0385) 44222

Location: Access from Ireshopeburn, Wearhead and Cows Hill

THE WATER:	408 acres. Altitude 1305 ft. Lodge facilities. WCs. Maximum number of rods per day: 10	
SEASON:	22 March to 30 September.	
HOURS:	6.00 a.m. to 7.00 p.m.	
		Price band (£)
COSTS:	Full rod (8 fish per day, 9 in. minimum size)	100.00 +
	OAP, disabled and children under 16	50.00 +
	Day ticket (8 fish, 9 in. minimum size)	4.00 +
	OAP, disabled and children under 16	2.00 +
	Weekly ticket	16.00 +
	Weekly OAP, disabled and child under 16	8.00 +
STOCKING POLICY:	Stocked with some browns.	
PERMITS:	No reservations required. Day permits available from lodge. Northumbrian Water Authority licence required, contact Wear Division (address above).	
GENERAL INFORMATION:	74 fish taken by 93 (recorded) rods. Worm or fly.	

BURRATOR RESERVOIR
Yelverton, Plymouth, Devon
Tel: (082 285) 2564

Location: Off B3212 from Yelverton

THE WATER:	150 acres.	
SEASON:	15 March to 30 September.	
HOURS:	Sunrise to midnight.	
		Price band (£)
COSTS:	Full rod (4 fish per day, 7 in. minimum size)	25.00–30.00
	Day ticket (4 fish, 7 in. minimum size)	1.75–2.50
	Concessionary tickets half-price.	
STOCKING POLICY:	Natural browns. Rainbows and brooks stocked as fry.	
PERMITS:	Reservations not required. Self-service machine. No water authority licence required.	
GENERAL INFORMATION:	Fly fishing and spinning. Dartmoor National Park. South West Water Authority.	

BUSHEY LEAZE
c/o Linch Hill Fishery, Stanton Harcourt, Oxon
Tel: Oxford (0865) 882 215

Location: Off the A361 north of Lechdale

THE WATER:	Season tickets only. 22 acres. Lodge facilities. Maximum number of rods per day: 40.
SEASON:	Mid-March to end of October. Winter season – 1 November to 3 January.
HOURS:	6.00 a.m. to one hour after sunset.
COSTS:	*Price band (£)* Full rod (8 fish per week/100 fish per season) 140.00–160.00 Mid-week Season (4 fish per week/50 fish per season) 105.00–125.00 Half-price for Junior tickets (under 16 years of age) *All above prices include VAT*
STOCKING POLICY:	Mainly rainbows. 100 fish per acre. Stocked twice monthly, or more, if required. 12 oz + with some larger fish.
PERMITS:	Members help themselves to up to six guest tickets per season at £8.00–9.00 per day; £6.00–7.00 per half day. Thames Water Authority licence required.
GENERAL INFORMATION:	Average: 50 fish per full rod per season. An annual barbeque and a dinner is organised by the members. Principally a traditional fly fishery. Special rules allow sinking lines only for first six weeks and last six weeks of the season. Very good hatches of mayfly and sedge. All flies to be tied on single hooks not exceeding size No. 6. All fish taken must exceed 12 in for rainbows and 14 in for browns. Undersized fish must be returned alive to the water.

CALVINGTON RESERVOIR
Howle, near Newport, Shropshire
Bailiff-Tel: Sambrook (095 279) 366

Location: Near A41. Near B5062. Near Newport

THE WATER:	$4\frac{1}{2}$ acres. Maximum number of rods per day: 30.	
SEASON:	Beginning March to end September.	
HOURS:	8.00 a.m. to sunset.	
		Price band (£)
COSTS:	Full rod	120.00–160.00
	Day ticket (4 fish)	6.00–7.50
	Evening ticket (2 fish)	4.00–5.00
PERMITS:	Reservations required.	

CAMELEY LAKES
Cameley, Temple Cloud, near Bristol, Avon
Tel: Temple Cloud (0761) 52790 or 52423

Location: Approximately 10 miles south of Bristol. About 1 mile off the A37 near Temple Cloud

THE WATER:	Three lakes of 2 acres, $1\frac{1}{2}$ acres and 1 acre. Lodge.	
SEASON:	Open all year.	
HOURS:	8.00 a.m. to sunset.	
		Price band (£)
COSTS:	Full rod	170.00–195.00
	Half rod	98.00–120.00
	Day ticket (4 fish)	7.00–8.50
STOCKING POLICY:	One lake exclusively browns.	
PERMITS:	Reservations required.	
GENERAL INFORMATION:	Fish average 2 lb. Dry fly/nymph only. Accommodation available. Winter weekends to include fishing, dinner, bed and breakfast. Casting/fly-tying tuition available.	

CHESTERFORD TROUT FISHERIES
T & H King Ltd., Bord Farm, Great Chesterford, Saffron Walden, Essex
Tel: Saffron Walden (0799) 30493

Location: Near M11 Junction 9, near A11

		Price band (£)
THE WATER:	Two lakes of 7 acres and 3 acres.	
SEASON:	Beginning April to mid-October	
HOURS:	9.00 a.m. to one hour past sunset.	
COSTS:	Day ticket (4 fish)	6.90–8.20
	Half-day ticket (2 fish)	3.50–4.75
PERMITS:	Reservations required.	

CHEW VALLEY LAKE
c/o Bristol Waterworks, Woodford Lodge, Chew Stoke, Bristol
Tel: Chew Magna (027 589) 2339

Location: 12 miles south of Bristol. Off A368 near junction with A38

THE WATER:	1,200 acres. Lodge facilities including main lounge, WC, drying room, tackle shop. Food available at picnic area shop. No limit to number of rods.
SEASON:	Early April to 15 October.
HOURS:	One hour before sunrise to one hour after sunset. Boat fishing from 10.00 a.m. to one hour after sunset.

Price band (£)

COSTS:	Full rod (covering Blagdon, Chew Valley Lake and the Barrows, 8 fish per day)	200.00–250.00
	Full rod (husband and wife) as above	350.00–425.00
	Full rod (OAP, disabled) Monday to Friday	110.00–150.00
	Full rod (juniors and full-time students)	85.00–110.00
	Day ticket (8 fish)	5.00–7.00
	Day ticket (OAP, disabled, juniors)	2.50–4.00

Prices inclusive of VAT and Wessex Water Authority licence fee.

BOATS:	Motor boats available. Maximum 3 fishermen per boat. Juniors must be accompanied by adult. Minimum fee for one rod in boat.
	Costs: £12.00–13.50 per day
	    £9.00–10.50 per day OAP, disabled, junior
	    Minimum fee for one rod using boat: £13.50–15.50

STOCKING POLICY:	Spring stocking followed by staggered restocking during season. All Bristol trout lakes: 100,000 brown and rainbow trout. Size 1 lb+ to 2 lb+. 50% browns, 50% rainbows.
PERMITS:	Reservations required for boat fishing only. Self-service kiosk for bank permits. No local waterboard licence required.
GENERAL INFORMATION:	17,641 fish caught during season. Average weight: 2 lb. Best brown: 8 lb. Best rainbow: 7.08 lb. 245 fish in 4 lb to 5 lb range. 33 fish in 5 lb to 6 lb range. 19 over 6 lb. Full rods are eligible for £3.00 reduction on cost of day boat and £1.50 after 3.00 p.m. Start season: Lures, sunk lines Late May/June: Smaller flies, floating lines Summer: floating lines, nymphs and small flies September: Floating lines, smaller flies

Late season: Sunk lines and lures

Accommodation is available in the area. Contact Bristol waterworks for list.

CHURCH HILL FARM
Mursley, Bucks
Tel: Mursley (029 672) 524

Location: off A413 Aylesbury-Buckingham Road. Near Whitchurch/Winslow. Off A421

THE WATER:	Dog Leg Lake of $2\frac{1}{2}$ acres and Jubilee Lake of $7\frac{1}{2}$ acres. Club house. WC. Hot lunches served every day except Sunday. A well-stocked shop carrying clothes, tackle and extensive range of flies. Maximum number of rods per weekday: 25. Maximum number of rods Saturday and Sunday: 30.
SEASON:	1 April to 31 October.
HOURS:	9.00 a.m. to 9.00 p.m. (or sunset).

Price band (£)

COSTS:		
	Day tickets (4 fish)	11.75–12.75
	Evening ticket (from 4.00 p.m., 2 fish)	6.00–7.00

Above prices include VAT.
Additional day tickets available.

STOCKING POLICY:	Stocking daily. Average weight: 2 lb with a good number of considerably larger fish also present. Rainbows and browns.
PERMITS:	Reservations advised. Anglian Water Authority licence required, available on premises.
GENERAL INFORMATION:	Average catch per rod is 2.4 fish. Lures generally most successful early and late season. Sedge patterns or shrimps do well after April up to September. The two lakes fish differently. The secret of success is altering tactics as may be required. Cottage at lake to let.

CLATWORTHY RESERVOIR
Taunton, Somerset
Tel: Wiveliscombe (0984) 23549
c/o Wessex Water Authority, Somerset Division, P.O. Box 9, King Square, Bridgwater
Tel: (0278) 57333

Location: Access via town of Wiveliscombe on A361 Taunton to Bampton Road. Edge of Exmoor

THE WATER:	130 acres. Lodge facilities. WC. No limit to number of rods per day.	
SEASON:	Beginning April to mid-October.	
HOURS:	8.00 a.m. until one hour after sunset.	
COSTS:		*Price band (£)*
	Full rod	80.00–100.00
	Day ticket (6 fish)	4.50–6.00
	Day ticket with boat (6 fish)	7.50–9.00
	Evening ticket with boat (after 4.00 p.m.)	5.50–7.00
	Junior, OAP approximately half price. Full rod permits available from Divisional Fisheries and Recreations Officer, Somerset Division (address above).	
BOATS:	Single occupancy OK (except opening weekend). Anchors provided. Boats may be booked in advance.	
STOCKING POLICY:	Stocking every 8–14 days. Usually between 75 to 100 fish per acre. Size between $1\frac{1}{4}$ lb to 2 lb. 75% rainbows, 25% browns.	
PERMITS:	No reservations required. Self-service kiosks for day tickets and boats. No water authority licence required.	
GENERAL INFORMATION:	30,000 fish stocked in total Wessex Water Authority reservoir area of 389 acres. 17,000 fish taken, from $1\frac{1}{2}$ lb to 4 lb.	

COD BECK RESERVOIR
c/o Yorkshire Water Authority, North Central Division, 'Spenfield', 182 Otley Road, Leeds
Tel: Leeds (0532) 448201

Location: Osmotherley, North Yorkshire

THE WATER:	24 acres. Maximum number of rods per day: 12.	
SEASON:	25 March to 30 September.	
HOURS:	8.00 a.m. to dusk.	
COSTS:	Day ticket (4 fish)	*Price band (£)* 2.00–2.50
	Tickets can be purchased from: Sub-Post Office, 4 West End, Osmotherley, North Yorkshire. Hours: Monday, Tuesday, Thursday, Friday: 9.00 a.m.–12.30 p.m. and 1.30 p.m.–5.30 p.m. Wednesday, Saturday: 9.00 a.m.–12.30 p.m.	
PERMITS:	Yorkshire Water Authority licence required for all anglers age 10 and over, available from Sub-Post Office (see above). Reservations required.	
GENERAL INFORMATION:	Any angler may apply for a permit, but preference given to persons residing in the area of supply of the Yorkshire Water Authority – North Central Division. Fly only.	

COLWICK PARK RESERVOIR
Off Mile End Road, Nottingham
Tel: Nottingham (0602) 247152
c/o STWA Office, Meadow Lane, Nottingham. Tel: Nottingham (0602) 865007

Location: Colwick, east of Nottingham. Off B686

THE WATER:	65 acres. Lodge facilities. Maximum number of rods per day: 110.
SEASON:	Mid-March to mid-October.
HOURS:	One hour before sunrise to one hour after sunset.

COSTS:		*Price band (£)*
	Full rod (4 fish per day)	100.00–125.00
	Day ticket High Season (4 fish)	4.20–5.50
	Day ticket Low Season (4 fish)	3.80–5.50
	Evening ticket	2.50–3.25
	Concessionary ticket (2 fish)	2.00–2.50

	Concessionary permits available for children under 16, disabled, OAP. Advance booking from STWA Office (address above). Permits from the fishing lodge, at the reservoir or The Tackle Box, Trent Bridge, Nottingham. Tel: (0602) 866121.

BOATS:	12 rowing boats available.
	Costs: £3.20–3.80 per day
	    £2.50–3.00 after 6.00 p.m.
	1 petrol outboard boat.
	Costs: £5.00–5.75 per day
	    £2.50–3.00 after 6.00 p.m.
	Boats available from 8.00 a.m. to half-hour after sunset.

STOCKING POLICY:	3,500 browns, 6,000 rainbows, 1,000 American brooks. 150 to the acre monthly restocking. 10–14+ inches.
PERMITS:	Severn-Trent Water Authority licence required, self-service facilities available.
GENERAL INFORMATION:	7,964 fish taken during season.

CONISTON WATER
Cumbria
c/o The National Trust, P.O. Box 30, Beckenham, Kent
No telephone

Location: Approached from Greenod on A590 — North to A5084

THE WATER:	$5\frac{1}{2}$ miles long.
SEASON:	March to September.
HOURS:	No restrictions.
COSTS:	No permit required. No limit to number of fish.
STOCKING POLICY:	Not stocked.
GENERAL INFORMATION:	Better known for the speed trials of 'Bluebird' than for its fishing, the water contains pike, perch, eels, trout and char.

COW GREEN RESERVOIR
Co. Durham
c/o Northumbrian Water Authority, Tees Division, Trenchard Avenue,
Thornaby, Stockton, Cleveland
Tel: Stockton (0642) 62216

*Location: Take the signposted road running west from the Langdon Beck
Hotel on the B6277 — the Alston to Middleton-in-Teesdale road*

THE WATER:	780 acres. Altitude 1,603 ft. Lodge facilities. WC. No limit to number of rods per day.
SEASON:	22 March to 30 September.
HOURS:	6.00 a.m. to 7.00 p.m.

Price band (£)

COSTS:	Day ticket (no bag limit, 9 in. minimum size)	2.00 +
	OAP, disabled, children under 16	1.00 +
PERMITS:	No reservations required. Self-service facilities for day tickets. Northumbrian Water Authority licence required, contact Tees Division (address above).	
GENERAL INFORMATION:	Worm or fly. Browns only. Not stocked. 1,802 fish taken by 1,589 (recorded) rods.	

CROMWELL TROUT LAKE
Cromwell, near Newark, Notts
Tel: Newark (0636) 812235

Location: North of Newark, Cromwell exit, west of A1

THE WATER:	20 acres.	
SEASON:	Mid-march to mid-November.	
HOURS:	8.00 a.m. to one hour after sunset.	
COSTS:		*Price band (£)*
	Day ticket (4 fish)	4.00–5.00
	Juniors (4 fish)	3.50–4.25
	(2 fish)	2.50–3.00

Day tickets available from Charlton Service Station – located on north-bound lane of A1, just past Cromwell Village turn-off, six miles north of Newark.

PERMITS: Reservations recommended at weekends. Severn-Trent Water Authority licence required.

GENERAL INFORMATION: More than 4,000 fish fell to slightly less than the same number of anglers – averaging not quite one fish per rod.

CROWN NETHERHALL TROUT FISHERY
Hoddesdon, Herts
Tel: Hoddesdon 43013 or 610408

Location: Off A1170, near A414 and A10. Dobb's Weir Road

THE WATER:	6 acres.	
SEASON:	1 March to 31 October.	
HOURS:	9.00 a.m. to one hour after sunset.	
		Price band (£)
COSTS:	Full rod	120.00–150.00
	Day ticket (weekdays, 4 fish)	5.50–7.00
	Day ticket (weekends, 4 fish)	6.50–8.25
PERMITS:	Reservations recommended. Permits from: Crown Fishery, Carthagena Lock, Broxbourne, Herts.	
GENERAL INFORMATION:	Fish mainly in the 1 lb range.	

CROXLEY HALL WATERS
Croxley Hall Farm, Rickmansworth, Herts
Tel: Rickmansworth 78290 or 72068

Location: Close to Rickmansworth, off A404, near A412, A4145. Near Croxley Underground station (Metropolitan line)

THE WATER:	Three lakes totalling $10\frac{1}{2}$ acres.	
SEASON:	1 April to end October.	
HOURS:	Day ticket: 9.00 a.m. to dusk Season ticket: 6.30 a.m. to dusk Closed Mondays.	
		Price band (£)
COSTS:	Full rod (weekday)	240.00–280.00
	Half rod	130.00–155.00
	Day ticket	10.50–12.00
	Evening ticket	5.50–6.50
STOCKING POLICY:	Stocked daily with rainbows, browns and brooks.	

DAMERHAM FISHERIES LIMITED
Damerham, South End, Fordingbridge, Hants.
Tel: Rockbourne (07253) 446

Location: From Fordingbridge take B3078 to Damerham (3 miles). Near Salisbury (14 miles)

THE WATER:	Six lakes totalling 17 acres plus 3 miles of bank fishing. Lodge. Some tackle available.
SEASON:	1 April to 31 October.
HOURS:	10.00 a.m. to dusk.

		Price band (£)
COSTS:	Full rod (4 fish per day)	286.00–320.00
	Half rod (4 fish per day)	155.00–180.00
	Day ticket (4 fish)	11.00–12.50
	Half day ticket (2 fish)	6.00–7.00

Additional day tickets available.

STOCKING POLICY:	Rainbows only, stocked regularly. $1\frac{1}{2}$ lb usual size. Some in the 6 lb to 10 lb range.
PERMITS:	Reservations recommended. No water authority licence required.
GENERAL INFORMATION:	A large mayfly hatch occurs annually.

DAMFLASK RESERVOIR

c/o Yorkshire Water Authority, West Riding House, Albion Street, Leeds
Tel: Leeds (0532) 448201

Location: At Low Bradfield, 6 miles north-west of Sheffield, South Yorkshire. Route via A616 and B6077

THE WATER:	115 acres. No lodge facilities. Chemical WCs situated around the reservoir. No limit to number of rods.	
SEASON:	25 March to 30 September.	
HOURS:	7.00 a.m. to dusk.	
		Price band (£)
COSTS:	Day ticket (2 fish, 11 in. minimum size)	1.50–2.25
	Half-day	.90–1.15
	Concessionary fishing tickets are available for juveniles aged up to and including 15 years. No additional day tickets available.	
STOCKING POLICY:	Stocking with browns and rainbows before commencement of season, then monthly throughout the season.	
PERMITS:	No reservations required. Day and half-day tickets are sold by ticket-dispensing machines at the reservoir. Yorkshire Water Authority licence required by all anglers 10 and above, not sold at reservoir.	

DARWELL RESERVOIR
Mountfield, near Robertsbridge, Sussex
Bailiff – Tel: Robertsbridge (0580) 880 407 for reservations (mornings)
Run by Hastings Flyfishers Club

Location: Off the A21 on the Robertsbridge to Battle road. Enter at Tunstall Farm

THE WATER:	180 acres.	
SEASON:	Beginning of April to end October.	
HOURS:	9.00 a.m. to one hour after sunset.	
COSTS:	Day ticket (6 fish)	*Price band (£)* 4.00–5.00
	Tickets available from bailiff between 9.00 a.m. and 10.00 a.m.	
BOATS:	Costs: £3.00–3.50 per day, for two rods.	
STOCKING POLICY:	Stocked as required throughout season. Rainbows and browns in the 1 lb range.	
PERMITS:	Reservations recommended. Southern Water Authority licence required, available from the bailiff.	

DEER SPRINGS
Stockeld, Wetherby, Yorks
Tel: Wetherby (0937) 63646

Location: Wetherby, off A1, A58

THE WATER:	1½ acres. Maximum number of rods per day: 3.	
SEASON:	No closed season.	
HOURS:	10.00 a.m. to dark.	
		Price band (£)
COSTS:	Day ticket (4 fish)	10.00–11.50
	Half day ticket (2 fish)	5.00–6.00
PERMITS:	Reservations required.	

DERWENT RESERVOIR
Edmundbyers, near Consett, Co. Durham
Tel: Consett (0207) 55250

Location: West of A68, at Junction with B6278

THE WATER:	1,000 acres. Lodge. WCs.	
SEASON:	1 May to mid-October.	
HOURS:	Bank: One hour before sunrise to one hour after sunset. Boat: 10.00 a.m. to sunset.	
COSTS:	Day ticket (8 fish)	*Price band (£)* 3.50–4.50
BOATS:	Rowing boats available. Costs: £6.50–7.50 per day Motor boats available. Costs: £13.00–15.00 per day	
STOCKING POLICY:	Rainbows in 1 lb range, browns 12 oz.	
PERMITS:	Reservations recommended for boats. Self-service for day tickets and boats.	
GENERAL INFORMATION:	Average about 1 fish per rod per visit. Further information: Sunderland and South Shields Water Co. 29 John Street, Sunderland. Tel: Sunderland (0783) 57123.	

DRAYCOTE RESERVOIR
Kites Hardwick, near Rugby, Warwickshire
Tel: Rugby (0788) 811107

Location: 5 miles south-west of Rugby. Near A426

THE WATER:	600 acres. Lodge facilities including mess room, hot drinks machine. WCs. Maximum number of rods per day: 300 bank and 64 boat anglers in 32 boats.	
SEASON:	Mid-April to end October.	
HOURS:	7.30 a.m. to one hour after sunset.	
COSTS:		Price band (£)
	Full rod (8 fish per day)	152.00–170.00
	Day ticket (8 fish)	5.20–6.50
	Evening ticket	3.10–4.00
	Concessionary ticket (4 fish)	2.50–3.25
	Concessionary tickets available for children under 16, disabled and OAP.	
	Permits and information from Fishing Lodge, Draycote Reservoir.	
BOATS:	Rowing boats available.	
	Costs: £3.80–4.75 per day	
	£2.50–3.00 after 4.00 p.m.	
	Petrol Outboard boats available.	
	Costs: £9.50–11.00 per day.	
	£5.00–6.00 after 4.00 p.m.	
	Reservations required. Boats available after 8.30 a.m. Single occupancy OK with permission of Senior Fishery Officer.	
STOCKING POLICY:	40,000 browns and rainbows during season on put-and-take basis, with 10,000 stocked before season begins.	
PERMITS:	Severn-Trent Water Authority licence required. Self-service facilities.	
GENERAL INFORMATION:	29,069 fish taken during season.	

DURLEIGH RESERVOIR
Bridgwater, Somerset
Tel: Bridgwater (0278) 424786

Location: 2 miles from Bridgwater. Best approached via West Street

THE WATER:	77 acres. Lodge facilities. WC. No limit to number of rods per day.	
SEASON:	End March to mid-October.	
HOURS:	8.00 a.m. until one hour after sunset.	
COSTS:		*Price band (£)*
	Full rod	80.00–105.00
	Day ticket (6 fish)	4.50–6.00
	Day ticket with boat (6 fish)	7.50–9.00
	Evening ticket with boat (after 4.00 p.m.)	5.50–7.00
	Junior, OAP approximately half price. Full rod permits available from Divisional Fisheries and Recreations Officer, Somerset Division (address above).	
BOATS:	Single occupancy OK (except opening weekend). Anchors provided. Boats may be booked in advance.	
STOCKING POLICY:	Stocking every 8–14 days. Usually between 75 to 100 fish per acre. Size: $1\frac{1}{4}$ to 2 lb. 75% rainbows, 25% browns.	
PERMITS:	No reservations required. Self-service kiosks for day tickets and boats. No water authority licence required.	
GENERAL INFORMATION:	30,000 fish stocked in total Wessex Water Authority reservoir area of 389 acres. 17,000 fish taken, from $1\frac{1}{2}$ lb to 4 lb.	

EAST BATSWORTHY FISHERY
Rackenford, Tiverton, Devon
Tel: Rackenford (088 488) 278

Location: Just off the B3221 about 12 miles from Tiverton, 7 miles from South Molton

THE WATER:	$1\frac{1}{2}$ acres. No lodge facilities. Maximum number of rods per day: 6.	
SEASON:	1 April to 30 September.	
HOURS:	Daylight to dusk.	
		Price band (£)
COSTS:	Day ticket (4 fish)	1.50–2.25
	Additional day ticket available at above price.	(plus additional cost for each fish taken)
STOCKING POLICY:	150 fish per acre, restocking weekly.	
PERMITS:	No reservations required. South West Water Authority licence required.	
GENERAL INFORMATION:	Average 2.25 fish per rod.	

EAST HANNINGFIELD HALL
East Hanningfield, near Chelmsford, Essex
Tel: Chelmsford (0245) 400 269

Location: Between the A130 and East Hanningfield

		Price band (£)
THE WATER:	2 acres.	
SEASON:	Mid-March to end October.	
HOURS:	8.00 a.m. to half-hour after sunset.	
COSTS:	Full rod	225.00–275.00
	Day ticket (4 fish)	8.00–10.00
	Half-day ticket (2 fish)	5.00–7.00
PERMITS:	Reservations recommended.	

EDGEFIELD HALL FARM
Edgefield, Melton Constable, North Norfolk
Tel: Holt (0206 371) 2437

Location: Off B1149 near Holt

THE WATER:	$5\frac{1}{2}$ acres.	
SEASON:	Beginning April to end October.	
HOURS:	8.00 a.m. to dark.	
		Price band (£)
COSTS:	Day ticket (4 fish)	6.00–7.50
	Evening ticket (2 fish)	4.00–4.75
GENERAL INFORMATION:	Self-catering accommodation available.	

ELINOR TROUT FISHERIES
Aldwincle, near Thrapston, Northants.
Tel: 0832 73671 for reservations after 7.30 p.m.

Location: Off A605 from Oundle, approximately 3 miles north of Thrapston

		Price band (£)
THE WATER:	40 acres. WC.	
SEASON:	1 April to end October.	
HOURS:	9.00 a.m. to dusk.	
COSTS:	Full rod	100.00–125.00
	Day ticket (4 fish)	4.00–5.00
	Additional day tickets available.	
BOATS:	Punts available. Costs: £2.00–2.50 per day.	
PERMITS:	Reservations recommended.	
GENERAL INFORMATION:	Free tuition can be provided.	

ELVINGTON LAKE
Lake Cottage, Wheldrake Lane, York
Tel: Elvington (090 485) 255

Location: Near A19/A64

THE WATER:	3 acres. Maximum number of rods per day: 40.	
SEASON:	Latter part of March to end February.	
HOURS:	6.30 a.m. to 9.00 p.m. or dusk.	
COSTS:	Day ticket	*Price band (£)* 1.50–2.00
	All fish caught must be returned to the water.	
STOCKING POLICY:	Stocked annually, as and when required. Rainbows up to 10 lb.	
PERMITS:	No reservations required. Yorkshire Water Authority licence required.	
GENERAL INFORMATION:	Please note: This lake also contains coarse fish, with a possibility that coarse fishermen may be encountered.	

EXE VALLEY FISHERY
Exebridge, Dulverton, Somerset
Tel: Dulverton (0398) 23328

Location: 3 miles south of Dulverton, 7 miles north of Tiverton. Off A396

THE WATER:	Two lakes of $\frac{1}{2}$ acre each. WC. Weighing-in room/shelter. Maximum number of rods per day: 10.
SEASON:	End March to end October.
HOURS:	8.00 a.m. to 9.00 p.m., or dusk (whichever is sooner).
COSTS:	Package payment. Price band: £2.00–3.00 for 4 fish or half-day. Fish charged at £1.00 per lb.
STOCKING POLICY:	Stocking daily. All rainbows. Average weight: 2.21 lb. Record: 15 lb.
PERMITS:	Reservations required. Local water board licence required.
GENERAL INFORMATION:	8,174 fish taken by 2,108 rods. No fish to be returned.

EYE BROOK RESERVOIR
Caldecott, Market Harborough, Leicestershire
Tel: Rockingham (053 670) 770264

Location: Entrance up a gated road opposite Caldecott Pumping Station, situated 100 yds along the Great Easton Road from Caldecott village

THE WATER:	406 acres. Lodge facilities. WCs. No limit to number of rods per day.
SEASON:	1 April to 30 September.
HOURS:	Dawn until one hour after sunset. Opening day, fishing commences at 8.00 a.m.

COSTS:		Price band (£)
	Full rod	135.00–150.00
	Day ticket	5.00–6.00
	Day ticket (after 5.00 p.m.)	2.50–3.25
	OAP/juvenile day ticket	2.00–2.50

No daily bag limit.

BOATS:	25 rowing boats available. Unaccompanied fishermen permitted. Three persons maximum: two fishing, one rowing. Reservations recommended. Anchors supplied. Fishermen allowed to use own electric outboard, fee 50p. Costs: £5.00–6.00 per day. £3.00–3.75 per evening.
STOCKING POLICY:	Stocked with 12 in+ browns and rainbows. Browns stocked pre-season, and until latter part of May, followed by rainbows. Stocking most weeks until early September. Usually about 30% browns, 70% rainbows.
PERMITS:	Reservations not required. Book of tickets and envelopes available at boat house. Fishermen to fill in with appropriate fee, place in box in booking-in room. Anglian Water Authority licence required, available at boathouse.
GENERAL INFORMATION:	26,140 fish taken by 18,478 rods. Early season bank fishing good. Favourite spots: Robo's Cabin to Harrisons Corner, the dam, the bell, cattle shed and chestnut. The following have proved to be fairly productive: April/May: Sweeney Todd, Butchers, Black & Peacock, Peter Ross, Alexandra, Black Chenille. July: Wickhams, Soldier Palmer, Greenwells, Invicta, Whisky Fly, Jersey Herd, brown and green nymphs, Eyebrook's Pheasant Tail. August/September: Nymphs Pheasant Tail, Red Nymph, Autumn Nymph, Baby Doll, Missionary

FARMIRE
Farnham, Knaresborough, N. Yorkshire
Tel: Harrogate (0423) 866417

Location: Near B6165/A6055. Near Knaresborough

THE WATER:	5 acres. Maximum number of rods per day: 10.	
SEASON:	Beginning April to beginning November.	
HOURS:	8.00 a.m. to 8.00 p.m.	
		Price band (£)
COSTS:	Full rod	175.00–210.00
	Day ticket (2 fish)	7.00–8.50
PERMITS:	Reservations required.	
GENERAL INFORMATION:	Barbless hook only permitted.	

FARMOOR 2 RESERVOIR
Cumnor Road, Farmoor, Oxford, Oxon
Tel: Cumnor (086 76) 3033

Location: Off B4017, near B4044/A420. Near Eynsham, Oxford

THE WATER:	240 acres. Lodge. Maximum number of rods per day: 150.
SEASON:	1 April to 30 November.
HOURS:	9.00 a.m. to half-hour after sunset.

COSTS:

	Price band (£)
Day ticket (weekday, 6 fish)	5.50–6.25
Day ticket (weekend, Bank Holiday, 6 fish)	6.00–6.75
Part-day ticket (weekday, 4 fish)	3.80–4.25
Part-day ticket (weekend, Bank Holiday, 4 fish)	4.30–4.75

Half-price for under 16s except for the first month of the season when the full price is charged.
Additional day tickets available, same prices as above.

STOCKING POLICY: About 80 fish per acre. Weekly stocking. Numbers stocked depend upon how well it is fishing. Aim to give average catch rate for the season of 1.5–2.0 fish per permit. No fish under 12 in stocked. Around 15% browns and 85% rainbows.

PERMITS: Reservations advised for first two weeks of season. Thames Water Authority licences required, available at gatehouse.

GENERAL INFORMATION: Thames Water Authority Reservoir.
28,059 trout taken by 15,206 anglers.
April/May: sinking line with most variations of black or white lures. Floating line mainly green, red and black buzzers.
June/July/August/September: mostly floating line or sink tip using most buzzer patterns and all stages of sedge imitations.
October/November: fry imitating lures on sinking lines; traditional wet flies on floating lines.
    The reservoir contours are similar throughout the fishing area. Feeding pattern mainly dependent on wind direction and food availability. Main types of food available are snail, shrimps, daphnia, chironomids, sedge, olives, crane fly, sticklebacks and fry.

FERNWORTHY RESERVOIR
Near Moretonhampstead, Devon.
Tel: Chagford (064 73) 2440

Location: Near A382/B3212

THE WATER:	76 acres. No lodge facilities. No limit to number of rods.	
SEASON:	1 May to 31 October.	
HOURS:	One hour before sunrise to one hour after sunset.	
COSTS:		*Price band (£)*
		Day ticket (5 fish) 4.50–6.00
	OAP, disabled, student under 18,	
	junior under 16	3.50–5.00
	Child under 14	1.00–1.50
	Evening (after 4.00 p.m., 3 fish)	2.50–3.50
	Book of 20 permits available at 15% discount. No additional day tickets available.	
BOATS:	Pulling boats available, seats 2. Anchors provided. No boats before 9.00 a.m. Costs: £4.50–5.50 per day. £3.00–3.50 half day (after 4.00 p.m.) Telephone Warden to book.	
STOCKING POLICY:	Pre-season stocking of brooks and rainbows, then trickle stocking throughout season with fish averaging over 1 lb.	
PERMITS:	No reservations required. Tickets on self-service, no change available. No local water authority licence required.	
GENERAL INFORMATION:	5,364 fish caught during season. 1.7 fish per rod day. This is a fishery that does extremely well with the use of teams of small flies which should invariably include either Black and Peacock Spider or a Black Gnat. Lure fishing need only be used during the very early season or when brilliant sun sends the fish deep.	
	South West Water Authority.	

FEWSTON RESERVOIR
c/o Yorkshire Water Authority, West Riding House, Albion Street, Leeds
Tel: Leeds (0532) 448 201

Location: Washburn Valley, West of Harrogate. Near Timble/Blubberhouses. Near A59

THE WATER:	156 acres.	
SEASON:	25 March to 30 September.	
HOURS:	7.00 a.m. to dusk.	
		Price band (£)
COSTS:	Day ticket (4 fish, 10 in. minimum size)	2.00–3.00
PERMITS:	No reservations required. Yorkshire Water Authority licence required by all anglers 10 and over.	
GENERAL INFORMATION:	Fly only.	

FISHERS GREEN
Crooked Mile, Holyfields, Waltham Abbey, Essex
Tel: 0992-763180 or Kings Langley (09972) 65772

Location: Waltham Abbey. Near A10 and A121. Off B194

THE WATER:	$4\frac{1}{2}$ acres. Hut/shelter. WC. Coffee/tea machine. Tackle, flies, leaders, available. Maximum number of rods per day: 20.
SEASON:	Late March to late November.
HOURS:	9.00 a.m. to dark.

COSTS:
	Price band (£)
Day ticket (4 fish)	9.00–10.25
Morning ticket (9.00 a.m.–1.00 p.m., 2 fish)	5.00–6.00
Evening ticket (5.30 p.m. to dark, 2 fish)	5.00–6.00

Junior, OAP, disabled – half price/half bag limit, with option of extension.
Additional day tickets available (maximum of 2), same price as above.

STOCKING POLICY:	150 fish per acre. Stocking daily at 1 lb to 7 lb. Average weight: 2 lb. 75% rainbows, 25% brooks and browns.
PERMITS:	Reservations required (see above phone numbers). Self-service vending machines. Thames Water Authority licence required, not available on premises.
GENERAL INFORMATION:	Maximum hook size No. 8 long shank. Single fly only.

FLOWERS FARM TROUT LAKES
Flowers Farm, Hillfield, Batcombe Down, Dorchester, Dorset
Tel: Cerne Abbas (030 03) 351

Location: Situated about half-way between Dorchester and Yeovil off A37, next to St. Francis Friary

THE WATER:	Three lakes of 2 acres, 1 acre and $\frac{1}{2}$ acre. Small lodge. A limited amount of tackle can be loaned. Maximum number of rods per day: 10.
SEASON:	Mid-March to 31 December.
HOURS:	5.30 a.m. to one hour after sunset.
COSTS:	*Price band (£)* Day ticket (4 fish) 7.50–8.50 Half-day ticket (3 fish) 6.00–7.00 Evening ticket (2 fish) 5.00–6.00 Additional tickets can be purchased.
STOCKING POLICY:	Stocked weekly. 200 fish per acre. Size range: 13 inches (1 lb) to 24 inches ($4\frac{1}{2}$ lb to 5 lb). 80% rainbows, 20% browns.
PERMITS:	Reservations preferred. No local water authority licence required.
GENERAL INFORMATION:	1,575 fish taken by 1,105 rods. Small flies – 10 downward. Black, early spring – fished deep. Nymphs later – slow-sink/floating-line. Summer: sedges. Autumn: nymphs, floating line.

FONTBURN RESERVOIR
Northumberland
Tel: Rothbury (0669) 20465
c/o Northumbrian Water Authority, Northumberland and Tyne Division, Northumbria House, Town Centre, Cramlington

Location: 5 miles south of Rothbury on B6324 Rothbury to Scouts Gap road. Access signposted

THE WATER:	87 acres. Altitude 610 ft. Lodge facilities. WC. No limit to number of rods per day. Other facilities in area.	
SEASON:	22 March to 30 September.	
HOURS:	6.00 a.m. to 7.00 p.m.	
		Price band (£)
COSTS:	Day ticket (no bag limit, 9 in minimum size)	2.00 +
	OAP, disabled, children under 16	1.00 +
PERMITS:	No reservations required. Self-service facilities for day tickets. Northumbrian Water Authority licence required, contact Northumberland and Tyne Division (address above).	
GENERAL INFORMATION:	Browns only. Unstocked. Worm or fly. 520 fish taken by 779 (recorded) rods.	

FOREMARK RESERVOIR
Near Burton-on-Trent, Derbyshire.
c/o Leicester Water Centre, Gorse Hill, Anstey, Leicester
Tel: Leicester (0533) 352011

Location: Near Burton-on-Trent/Derby/Ashby. Off A514

THE WATER:	230 acres. Lodge facilities. WC. No limit to number of rods per day.	
SEASON:	End April to mid-October.	
HOURS:	7.00 a.m. to half-hour after sunset.	
		Price band (£)
COSTS:	Full rod (6 fish per day)	125.00–150.00
	Day ticket High Season (6 fish)	4.60–6.00
	Day ticket Low Season (6 fish)	4.20–5.50
	Concessionary day ticket (3 fish)	2.20–3.00
	Concessionary permits available for children under 16, disabled, OAP. Permits available from Bendalls Farm Shop, adjacent to entrance of reservoir. Tel: (0283) 703294. Season permits from Leicester Water Centre (address above).	
BOATS:	Rowing boats available from 8.00 a.m. Boats may be reserved. Cost: £3.80–4.75.	
STOCKING POLICY:	5,000 browns, 12,000 rainbows and 3,000 American brooks.	
PERMITS:	Severn-Trent Water Authority licence required.	
GENERAL INFORMATION:	19,474 fish caught during season. No fly or lure exceeding 2 in. in length and bearing more than one single hook may be used.	

FRENSHAM TROUT LAKE
Wishanger Stud, Frensham Lane, Churt, Surrey
Tel: Frensham (025 125) 4170.

Location: 5 miles from Farnham, Surrey. Proceed to Frensham Pond Hotel, drive up Bacon Lane, fork right to Frensham Lane, proceed for 1 mile. See Wishanger Stud on right-hand side. Also, approximately 5 miles from Hindhead, taking Farnham Road from Hindhead which is situated on A3 from London-Portsmouth Road

THE WATER:	Approximately 2 acres (set in 50 acres of countryside). Approximately 500 yards of River Wey (single bank). Fishing Lodge adjacent to lake. Tackle available for hire or purchase. Large stock of flies. Food and flasks of tea available. Maximum number of rods per day: 5–7.
SEASON:	March to November.
HOURS:	8.00 a.m. until dusk.

COSTS:		Price band (£)
	Full rod (4 fish)	140.00–160.00
	Day ticket (4 fish)	9.00–10.50
	Evening ticket (2 fish)	5.00–6.00

Children: 25% rate reduction.
Additional day tickets available. Cost reduction 30%.

BOATS:	One boat available (maximum of 2 in boat). Anchor provided. Cost: £2.00.
STOCKING POLICY:	Stocking 150 fish per acre on a regular basis. Size range: 1 lb to 9 lb. 90% rainbows, 10% browns.
PERMITS:	Telephone reservations preferred. Day tickets available at The Lodge (Main House). No local water board licence required.
GENERAL INFORMATION:	Of 200 anglers only about one dozen failed to take their limit. Summer months, fish deeper water. Lake fairly well sheltered from wind. No real change by weather conditions. No lure fishing. Bed and breakfast available on premises.

GAILEY TROUT FISHERY
Gailey Lea Lane, Penkridge, near Cannock, Staffs
Lodge – Tel: Penkridge (078 571) 4855

Location: near M6, Junction 12. Near A5, near Cannock

THE WATER:	37 acres. Lodge.	
SEASON:	1 March to 31 October.	
HOURS:	9.00 a.m. to dusk.	
		Price band (£)
COSTS:	Day ticket (4 fish)	7.00–8.50
	Evening ticket (2 fish)	4.00–5.00
BOATS:	Costs: £2.50–3.00 per person per day.	
	£2.00–2.50 per person per evening.	
STOCKING POLICY:	Stocked weekly. 100 fish per acre.	
PERMITS:	Reservations recommended. Advance bookings from: Mrs. G. Brassington, Dunromin, Woodlands Lane, Hatherton, Cannock Tel: Cannock (05435) 4760. (Enclosing fee and SAE – cheques payable to Gailey Trout Fishery.)	

GRAFHAM WATER
West Perry, Huntingdon, Cambridgeshire
Manager's Office – Tel: Huntingdon (0480) 810247. Fishing Lodge – Tel: Huntingdon (0480) 810531

Location: Approximately 1½ miles west of Buckden roundabout on the A1 between Huntingdon and St. Neots

THE WATER:	1,570 acres. Fishing lodge offers rod room, WCs, lounge. Tackle sold includes flies, monofilament, flylines and basses. No limit to number of rods per day. Over 8 miles of shoreline available for fishing.	
SEASON:	Open last Saturday in April to next to last Sunday in October.	
HOURS:	One hour before sunrise to one hour after sunset.	

		Price band (£)
COSTS:	Full rod (8 fish per day)	190.00–210.00
	Weekday season (8 fish per day)	145.00–160.00
	Seven day ticket (8 fish per day)	27.50–33.50
	Day ticket (8 fish)	5.50–7.00
	Evening ticket	3.50–4.25

Junior tickets available half price.
No second ticket available.

BOATS:	37 boats, with or without outboard motors. To be occupied by a minimum of two people. Booking not essential, but recommended, especially at weekends. Anchors not provided, though flotation cushions and drogues are. Costs: Motor boat: £13.00–15.00 per day; £8.00–9.50 per evening. Rowing boat: £7.00–8.00 per day; £4.00–5.00 per evening.
STOCKING POLICY:	Stocking annually, starting before season, continuing at regular intervals. 62,000 fish were introduced, 12–13 in. average. Browns average about 10% of total.
PERMITS:	Reservations not required. Vending machine for day and evening tickets (adult only). Anglian Water Authority licence required, available at Lodge.
GENERAL INFORMATION:	57,466 fish caught, as recorded from 16,847 returns. (It is impossible to state exactly the number of rod visits as there are no statistics for season ticket holders.) A fairly exposed lake, can be subject to strong winds from nearly all quarters, though many boat anglers prefer blustery conditions. Early on and late in the season fishing below the surface, with a lure, can produce results. As water temperatures go up, more takes will be had to rising

fish. Chironomid hatches occur during the middle of the season, and the use of buzzers and nymphs then comes into its own. A popular spot with a lot of bank anglers is the dam wall, because of the deep water and ease of access. However, a lot of tackle can be lost on the back-cast.

A force 6 wind from the north makes the launching of boats hazardous and, at times, nigh on impossible. Under these conditions boat fishing may be curtailed.

GRASSHOLME RESERVOIR
Co. Durham
c/o Northumbrian Water Authority, Tees Division, Trenchard Avenue, Thornaby, Stockton, Cleveland
Tel: Stockton (0642) 62216

Location: Off B6218 near Middleton-in-Teesdale/Mickleton

THE WATER:	250 acres. Altitude 903 ft. Lodge facilities. WC. No limit to number of rods per day.	
SEASON:	22 March to 30 September.	
HOURS:	6.00 a.m. to 7.00 p.m.	
		Price bands (£)
COSTS:	Full rod (8 fish, 9 in. minimum size)	100.00 +
	OAP, disabled and children under 16	50.00 +
	Day ticket (8 fish, 9 in. minimum size)	4.00 +
	OAP, disabled and children under 16	2.00 +
	Weekly ticket	16.00 +
	OAP, disabled and children under 16	8.00 +
BOATS:	Rowing boats available from 8.30 a.m. for two anglers. May be reserved. Costs: £5.00 + per day; £3.00 + per evening.	
STOCKING POLICY:	Browns only.	
PERMITS:	No reservations required. Self-service facilities for day tickets. Northumbrian Water Authority licence required, contact Tees Division (address above).	
GENERAL INFORMATION:	Worm or fly. 7,407 fish taken by 5,083 (recorded) rods. Accommodation, camping, caravan site available nearby.	

GREENFIELD LAKE
Buckden, near Skipton, N. Yorkshire
Tel: Skipton (0756) 76858

Location: Leave A684 towards Buckden

THE WATER:	$2\frac{1}{2}$ acres. Maximum number of rods per day: 10.	
SEASON:	End March to end September.	
HOURS:	Sunrise to sunset.	
COSTS:		*Price band (£)*
	Day ticket (4 fish)	4.50–6.00
	Evening ticket	3.50–5.50
PERMITS:	Reservations recommended.	
GENERAL INFORMATION:	300–400 fish taken from the water during season. Wild fish in existence, able to use feeder springs for spawning.	

HANNINGFIELD WATER
c/o Essex Water Company, Hanningfield Works, South Hanningfield,
Chelmsford, Essex
Tel: Chelmsford (0245) 400381
Fishing lodge – Tel: Basildon (0268) 710101

Location: Between West Hanningfield and South Hanningfield, 6 to 8 miles south of Chelmsford. Main road access is from A130 Chelmsford to Southend road, or A129/A132 Billericay to Wickford road. The fishing lodge is in South Hanningfield, down a narrow lane marked 'No Through Road' off the South Hanningfield to Wickford road

THE WATER:	874 acres. Roughly 560 acres are open to boat fishing. Three miles of bank fishing. Lodge facilities available. Changing rooms, WCs, rest room. Maximum number of rods per day: 300 (Season only).
SEASON:	29 April to 29 October.
HOURS:	Bank fishing from 8.00 a.m. until one hour after sunset.

		Price band (£)
COSTS:	(300) Full rod (6 fish per day)	255.00–290.00
	(170) Weekday only (6 fish per day)	185.00–210.00

Above prices include VAT

BOATS:	Rowing boats available from 9.00 a.m. Three persons maximum: two fishing, one rowing. £7.00–8.50 per day. £4.00–5.00 half day. £2.25–2.75 per evening.
STOCKING POLICY:	50,000 trout, about half stocked during months of February and March, the rest as staggered plantings throughout June to September. Average size: 12 in. +, to 1 lb weight. 90% rainbows, 10% browns. 57 trout to the acre.
PERMITS:	Season permits only, no day tickets. Essex River Division Rod Licence required.
GENERAL INFORMATION:	36,221 fish taken by 16,544 anglers. 2.19 fish per rod visit. Average weight: 1 lb 9½ oz. 　Sunk lines and lures are favoured at start and end of season. Switch to nymphs and sedge imitations on floating line during summer. Boat anglers catch more fish than bank anglers to the ratio of 3 to 2 on average, but the bigger fish are caught by the bank angler, especially from the dam wall. Anglian Water Authority.

HAWKRIDGE RESERVOIR
Bridgwater, Somerset
c/o Wessex Water Authority, P.O. Box 9, King Square, Bridgwater
Tel: (0278) 57333

Location: Quantock Hills. 6 miles west of Bridgwater, just beyond Spaxton village

		Price band (£)
THE WATER:	32 acres. Lodge facilities. WC. No limit to number of rods per day.	
SEASON:	Beginning April to mid-October.	
HOURS:	8.00 a.m. until one hour after sunset.	
COSTS:	Full rod	65.00–80.00
	Day ticket (6 fish)	4.50–6.00
	Junior, OAP approximately half price. Full rod permits available from Divisional Fisheries and Recreations Officer, Somerset Division (address above).	
STOCKING POLICY:	Stocking every 8–14 days. Usually between 75 to 100 fish per acre. Average size: $1\frac{1}{4}$ lb to 2 lb. 75% rainbow, 25% browns.	
PERMITS:	No reservations required. Self-service kiosks for day tickets. No water authority licence required.	
GENERAL INFORMATION:	30,000 fish stocked in total Wessex Water Authority reservoir area of 389 acres. 17,000 fish taken, from $1\frac{1}{2}$ lb to 4 lb.	

HIGHAM FARM TROUT FISHERY
Old Higham, near Alfreton, Derbyshire
Tel: Alfreton (077 383) 3812/3

Location: On B6013, off the A61 Derby to Sheffield road. 3 miles from Alfreton, 5 miles from M1 Junction 28

THE WATER:	12 acres. Hotel, restaurant.	
SEASON:	1 April to mid-October.	
HOURS:	Dawn till dusk.	
		Price band (£)
COSTS:	Full rod	180.00–220.00
	Half rod	90.00–110.00
	Day ticket	10.00–12.50
	Daily catch limit: 2 rainbows/2 browns	
PERMITS:	Reservations recommended.	
GENERAL INFORMATION:	Anglers are permitted to land up to 8 fish, 4 of which may be retained.	

HILL VIEW TROUT LAKE
Skegness Road, Hogsthorpe, near Skegness, Lincolnshire
Tel: Skegness (0754) 72979

Location: A52 road Hogsthorpe $\frac{1}{2}$ mile on the south side of the village. 7 miles from Skegness; 9 miles from Mablethorpe

THE WATER:	2 acres. Tackle for sale and hire. Refreshments. Maximum number of rods per day: 25.	
SEASON:	1 April to 29 October inclusive.	
HOURS:	10.00 a.m. to dusk.	
		Price band (£)
COSTS:	Day ticket (4 fish)	5.00–6.50
	Half-day ticket (2 fish)	3.50–4.50
	One additional day ticket available, same price as above.	
STOCKING POLICY:	Lake stocked weekly mainly with rainbows from 1 lb to 12 lb, approximately 5% browns.	
PERMITS:	Reservations required only on opening and closing days. Day tickets purchased at Warden's Caravan. Anglian Water Authority licence required.	
GENERAL INFORMATION:	Catch rate averages just under 2 fish per rod. Best flies: April and May: Jersey Herd, Sweeney Todd, Appetiser, Baby Doll, Black Lure, Black and Peacock Spider. June, July, August: Pheasant Tail Nymph, Green and Black Buzzers, Dry Olives and Sedges. September and October: Shrimp Fly, Stick Fly, Polystickle and Muddler Minnow. Good evening rises from June to September. No dogs allowed.	

HORSESHOE LAKES
Wildmoorway Lane, South Cerney, near Cirencester, Gloucester
Office – Tel: Penn (049481) 2555
Fishery – Tel: Cirencester (0285) 861034

Location: On the outskirts of the village of South Cerney, within the Cotswold Water Park. Off A419

THE WATER:	Two lakes of 14 acres and 12 acres. Lodge. Flies and basic tackle available. Maximum number of rods per day: 80.	
SEASON:	Mid-March to end January.	
HOURS:	7.00 a.m. to dusk	
COSTS:		*Price band (£)*
	Full rod (4 fish per day)	220.00–250.00
	Half rod	112.00–130.00
	Day ticket (4 fish)	8.50–9.75
	Evening ticket	4.50–5.50
	Junior Day tickets (2 fish)	4.50–5.50
	Additional day tickets available, same price as above.	
STOCKING POLICY:	Daily stocking. Fish from $1\frac{1}{2}$ lb average to 15 lb.	
PERMITS:	Reservations required for weekends and bank holidays. Thames Water Authority licence required, available at the lodge.	
GENERAL INFORMATION:	Average number of fish per rod: 2.6. Most successful fly patterns: Pheasant Tail Nymph, Damosel Nymph, Mayfly Nymph, Viva, Horseshoe Fly, Appetiser. Regular casting clinics available for beginners and for those wishing to improve their casting technique. No. 6 hook maximum size. Up to three flies per cast allowed, no tandem lures, no double or treble hooks.	

HUCKLESBROOK TROUT LAKES
Fordingbridge, Hants
Tel: Cranborne (07254) 505 or Ringwood (04254) 3091

Location: On A338 north of Ringwood and south of Fordingbridge

THE WATER:	25 acres. Tackle and fly dressing shop. Rod and tackle hire. Maximum number of rods per day: 40.
SEASON:	1 April to 30 September.
HOURS:	9.00 a.m. to 8.00 p.m., or sunset, whichever comes first.
COSTS:	*Price band (£)* Full rod (one weekend day per week, 4 fish) 200.00–230.00 Full rod (one weekday per week, 4 fish) 175.00–200.00 Day ticket (4 fish) 6.75–7.50 Half-day ticket (2 fish) 4.00–5.00 Additional day tickets available. All prices include VAT and Water Authority Licence.
BOATS:	Four boats available accommodating 1 to 2 anglers. Costs: £2.50–3.00 per day.
STOCKING POLICY:	Average 80 fish per acre. Stocking takes place about five times per year, not necessarily during season. Fish are from 1 lb to 6 lb. Approximately 80% rainbows, 15% American brooks and 5% browns.
PERMITS:	Reservations strongly recommended.
GENERAL INFORMATION:	Fishing from anchored boats only. Tuition in casting and fly dressing available.

HURY RESERVOIR
Co. Durham
c/o Northumbrian Water Authority, Tees Division, Trenchard Avenue, Thornaby, Stockton, Cleveland
Tel: Stockton (0642) 62216

Location: Balderdale, about 2 miles from the village of Cotherstone. Near Barnard Castle

THE WATER:	204 acres. Altitude 860 ft. Lodge facilities. WC. No limit to number of rods per day.	
SEASON:	22 March to 30 September.	
HOURS:	6.00 a.m. to 7.00 p.m.	
		Price band (£)
COSTS:	Full rod (8 fish, 9 in. minimum size)	100.00 +
	OAP, disabled and children under 16	50.00 +
	Day ticket (8 fish, 9 in. minimum size)	4.00 +
	OAP, disabled and children under 16	2.00 +
	Weekly ticket	16.00 +
	OAP, disabled and children under 16	8.00 +
BOATS:	Rowing boats available for 2 anglers. May be reserved. Available from 8.30 a.m. Costs: £5.00 + per day. £3.00 + per evening.	
STOCKING POLICY:	Browns only.	
PERMITS:	No reservations required. Self-service facilities for day tickets. Northumbrian Water Authority licence required, contact Tees Division (address above).	
GENERAL INFORMATION:	Worm or fly. 4,935 fish taken by 3,034 (recorded) rods.	

JOHN O'GAUNTS
Kings Somborne, Hampshire
Reservations: Jasmine Cottage, Kings Somborne, Stockbridge, Hampshire
Tel: Kings Somborne (07947) 353

Location: Off A3057

		Price band (£)
THE WATER:	5 acres.	
SEASON:	Early April to mid-October.	
HOURS:	9.00 a.m. to one hour after sunset.	
COSTS:	Day ticket (4 fish)	8.00–10.00
	Half-day ticket	4.00–5.50
PERMITS:	Reservations recommended.	

KEMPTON PARK (WEST) RESERVOIR
Feltham Hill Road, Hanworth, Middlesex
Tel: 01-837 3300 and ask for Kempton Park

Location: Near A305, A308. Near Hanworth, Feltham Hill, Kempton Park Railway station

THE WATER:	21 acres. Lodge. WCs. Maximum number of rods per day: 10 boat anglers and 40 bank anglers.
SEASON:	Mid-March to end November.
HOURS:	7.30 a.m. or sunrise (whichever is later) to half-hour after sunset.

		Price band (£)
COSTS:	Day ticket (weekdays, 6 fish)	5.60–6.25
	Day ticket (weekends/bank holidays, 6 fish)	7.20–8.00
	Half-day ticket (weekdays, 4 fish)	4.00–4.50
	Half-day ticket (weekends/Bank holidays, 4 fish)	5.60–6.25
	All prices include VAT	

	Half price for under-16s except for first month of season when full price is charged. Additional day tickets available, same price as above.
BOATS:	Five rowing boats available for one or two anglers. Costs: Weekdays: £3.30–3.75 per day; £2.50–2.80 part day Weekends/Bank holidays: £4.40–5.00 per day; £3.30–3.75 part day.
STOCKING POLICY:	About 100 fish per acre. Two, three times week stocking. Aim to give average catch rate for the season of 1.5–2.0 fish per permit. No fish under 12 in. stocked. Nearly all rainbows; small number of browns.
PERMITS:	Reservations advised first week of season. Thames Water Authority licence required, available at reservoir.
GENERAL INFORMATION:	9,380 trout taken by 4,938 anglers. Reservoir is more or less square and approximately 15–20 ft deep. Banks are fairly gentle sloping with deepest part (and fish) out in the centre, hence boat fishing more successful than bank. March, April: Middle of the day favours bright lures, darker ones early and late. Often lures that do well in the morning will not produce in the afternoon. May is a 'Jekyll and Hyde' month, depending upon whether spring is early or late. Red and amber nymphs; Whisky, Baby Doll, Sweeney Todd lures.

June to September: Black and Peacock, Butcher, Invicta, Black Palmer in early morning; nymphs, mid and late morning. Toward dusk, fishing just below the surface with wet flies.

September onwards: The major item will be sticklebacks, use flashy lures, with silver and red.

Thames Water Authority Reservoir.

KENNICK AND TOTTIFORD RESERVOIR
Near Bovey Tracey, Devon
Tel: Bovey Tracey (0626) 833199 or Christow (0647) 52138

Location: Near the A382 and B3212

THE WATER:	Kennick: 45 acres, Tottiford: 35 acres. No lodge facilities. No limit to number of rods.	
SEASON:	1 April to 31 October.	
HOURS:	One hour before sunrise to one hour after sunset.	
COSTS:		*Price band (£)*
	Day ticket (5 fish)	4.50–6.00
	OAP, disabled, student under 18, junior under 16	3.50–5.00
	Child under 14	1.00–1.50
	Evening (after 4.00 p.m., 3 fish)	2.50–3.50
	Book of 20 permits available at 15% discount. No additional day tickets available.	
STOCKING POLICY:	Pre-season stocking of browns and rainbows, then trickle stocking throughout season with fish averaging over 1 lb.	
PERMITS:	No reservations required. Tickets on self-service, no change available. No local water authority licence required.	
GENERAL INFORMATION:	10,731 fish caught during season. 1.8 fish per rod day.	

Black lures prove very successful early season, and the success of lures continues throughout the season when the sun is bright although colour emphasis changes to yellow and white.

Nymphing and dry fly fishing very successful at these reservoirs with hatches throughout the season starting with Hawthorns in late April/early May followed by hatches of sedge, alder, buzzers and daddy longlegs at the end.

Recommended flies include Black and Peacock Spider, Butchers, Greenwell's Glory, Invictas, Ginger Quills, green and black buzzers, Black Gnat.

South West Water Authority

KIELDER WATER
c/o Northumbrian Water Authority, Northumbrian House, Regent Centre, Newcastle-upon-Tyne
Tel: Gosforth (0632) 843151

Location: Off the B6320 at Bellingham in the direction of Falstone

THE WATER:	2,684 acres. Lodge. Picnic sites. Caravan site. WCs.	
SEASON:	From 1 June.	
HOURS:	6.00 a.m. to one hour after sunset.	
COSTS:		*Price band (£)*
	Full rod	100.00–120.00
	Castabout	150.00–175.00
	Day ticket (8 fish)	4.00–5.00
	Junior tickets about half price.	
BOATS:	Rowing boats and motor boats. Not available to single anglers.	
PERMITS:	Self service facilities available. Water Authority licence not required.	

KINGSBRIDGE LAKES
57 Dorchester Road, Lytchett Minster, Poole, Dorset
Tel: Lytchett Minster (0202) 622220

Location: Organford turn-off A35 Poole to Dorchester road, just west of 'Bakers Arms' roundabout. Past post office, over small bridge and 200 yards on left turn down signposted lane

THE WATER:	Two lakes: rainbow only, approximately 5–6 acres; brown and rainbow, approximately 1 acre. Lodge. WCs. Hot drinks, snacks. Tackle and flies for purchase or rent. Maximum number of rods per day: 17.
SEASON:	24 March to early January.
HOURS:	8.30 a.m. to half-hour past sunset (or 9.00 p.m., whichever is earlier).

COSTS:		*Price band (£)*
	Full rod	192.00–215.00
	Half rod	102.00–125.00
	Day ticket	8.00–9.50
	Special day ticket	5.00–6.00
	All prices include VAT.	

Note: Catch and release. May keep up to two fish on regular day ticket. No fish included on special day ticket. Extra fish may be taken at £1.00 per pound.

STOCKING POLICY:	Approximately 200 to the acre. Restocked as caught. New stock 2–3 times per week. Average size: 1 lb 14 oz. Rainbows to 13 lb, browns to $8\frac{1}{2}$ lb.
PERMITS:	Reservations advisable. Wessex Water Authority licence required.
GENERAL INFORMATION:	Average: 1.65 caught and killed. 3.85 caught and returned. Ace of Spades, Whiskey Fly, Appetizer, Pheasant Tail, Damsel Fly, Buzzer. Both trout lakes fairly deep. Minimum 5 lb breaking strain leader recommended. Record rainbow: 9 lb 1 oz. Record brown: 5 lb 1 oz. Record catch: 23. Barbless hooks required, size No. 8 maximum.

KING'S LANGLEY TROUT FISHERY
King's Langley, Herts.
Tel: King's Langley 69863 or 63972

Location: On A41 — South part of town — turn east on road opposite Rose & Crown pub, Church Lane. Proceed through yard to car park

THE WATER:	$4\frac{1}{2}$ acres. Lodge. WC. Coffee, tea, snacks. Tackle, flies. Maximum number of rods per day: 20.	
SEASON:	End March to mid-November.	
HOURS:	9.00 a.m. to dusk.	
		Price band (£)
COSTS:	Day ticket (5 fish)	10.00–11.00
	Morning ticket (2 fish)	5.00–6.00
	Evening ticket (2 fish)	5.00–6.00
	Special rates for young people by arrangement. Additional day tickets available.	
STOCKING POLICY:	150 fish per acre. Fish in the 2 lb range, average.	
PERMITS:	Reservations recommended. Thames Water Authority licence required.	
GENERAL INFORMATION:	3,000 + fish taken by approximately 2,300 rods.	

LADYBOWER RESERVOIR
Ashopton Road, Bamford, near Sheffield, North Derbyshire
Tel: Hope Valley (0433) 51254
c/o STWA Office, Bamford, near Sheffield
Tel: (0433) 4424

Location: In Peak District of North Derbyshire on A57 between Sheffield and Manchester. Near village of Bamford

THE WATER:	504 acres. Lodge facilities. No limit to the number of rods per day.	
SEASON:	Early April to mid-October.	
HOURS:	One hour before sunrise to one hour after sunset.	
COSTS:		*Price band (£)*
	Full rod	85.00–100.00
	Day ticket High Season	4.50–5.50
	Day ticket Low Season	4.00–5.00
	Evening ticket	2.75–3.50
	Concessionary ticket	2.25–2.75
	Four fish per day up to end of May, thereafter, 6 fish. Evening: 3 fish till end of May, thereafter, 4 fish. Concessionary permits available for children under 16, disabled, OAP. Bag limits half normal for fishery. Additional permits available. Permits from Fishery Office, Ladybower Reservoir,. Advance booking and permits from STWA Office (address above) or STWA Office, Dimple Road, Matlock. Tel: (0629) 55051.	
BOATS:	Nine rowing boats available. 1 or 2 fishermen per boat. Phone reservations recommended. Anchors provided. Costs: £3.80–4.75 per day £2.50–3.00 after 4.00 p.m.	
STOCKING POLICY:	24,000 browns, rainbows and brooks stocked throughout season.	
PERMITS:	Reservations not required. Severn-Trent Water Authority licence required.	
GENERAL INFORMATION:	14,738 fish taken by 7,025 rods. No fly or lure exceeding 2 in. in length and bearing more than one single hook may be used. Fishery office open 10.00 a.m. daily.	

LADYWELL LAKES TROUT FISHERY
Arle House, Ladywell Lane, Alresford, Hants
Tel: Alresford (096 273) 2317

Location: A31. 7 miles from Winchester. Entrance to fishery is from The Dean

THE WATER:	Three lakes totalling 2½ acres with a short run of chalk stream. Locally recommended flies are available in fishing hut.	
SEASON:	Beginning April to 30 September. Closed on Tuesdays.	
HOURS:	9.00 a.m. to dusk.	

		Price band (£)
COSTS:	Full rod (4 fish per day)	185.00–220.00
	Half rod (4 fish per day)	98.00–120.00
	Day ticket (4 fish)	9.00–11.00
	Half day ticket (2 fish)	5.00–6.50
	Extra brace	4.50–6.00

Additional day ticket available.

STOCKING POLICY:	One lake browns only. Other two lakes predominantly rainbows. Restocking at frequent intervals throughout season. Stocking with fish not less than 12 in. Average: 1 lb 6 oz.
PERMITS:	No water board licence required. Reservations required.
GENERAL INFORMATION:	1,736 fish taken by 647 rods. Average 2.7 fish per rod visit. Tuition with tackle provided for beginners. Most successful flies are black, brown and green nymphs, Corixa, Pheasant Tail Nymph, Buzzers, Yellow Sally and various small whitish flies. One fly only. Maximum hook size No. 8 and length not exceeding ¾ in.

LAKE WINDERMERE
South Lakeland District Council, Ashleigh, Windermere, Cumbria.
Tel: Windermere (09662) 2244

Location: From Kendal — A5284 — north on A591, through Staveley to Windermere town

THE WATER:	$10\frac{1}{2}$ miles long.
SEASON:	March to September.
HOURS:	No restrictions.
COSTS:	No charge, no limit.
STOCKING POLICY:	Not stocked.
GENERAL INFORMATION:	Pike, perch, trout, char. Few trout fishermen consider this water a serious venue. No restrictions on methods.

LAKEDOWN TROUT FISHERY
2 Oakenwood Cottages, Holmshurst Farm, Burwash Common, Sussex
Tel: West Burwash (04357) 449

Location: 7 miles from Tunbridge Wells

THE WATER:	Three lakes totalling 12 acres. WCs. Maximum number of rods per day: 25.	
SEASON:	Beginning April to end October.	
HOURS:	9.00 a.m. to dusk.	
COSTS:		*Price band (£)*
	Day ticket	10.00–12.00
	Half day ticket	5.00–6.00

First 4 lb of fish included in day ticket price. Payment required beyond that by the lb. Total of 8 fish may be taken. Additional day ticket available after 8 fish have been taken.

STOCKING POLICY:	Maintained at 150 fish per acre.
PERMITS:	Reservations recommended.
GENERAL INFORMATION:	Fish not required may be returned to the water. Only hooks size No. 10 or smaller permitted.

LATIMER PARK LAKES
Latimer, Chesham, Bucks
Tel: Little Chalfont (02404) 2396

Location: On B485 between Chesham and Chenies. Near Amersham/Little Chalfont. Off A404. 3 miles from North Orbital Road

THE WATER:	Two lakes of 8 and 4 acres. Lodge facilities. Limited selection of tackle, free tea and coffee, washing facilities. WC.
SEASON:	Beginning April to 30 September. Closed Sundays.
HOURS:	Season rod: 6.00 a.m. until dark Day ticket: 9.00 a.m. until dark Evening ticket: April and September: 4.00 p.m. to dark May to August: 5.00 p.m. to dark

COSTS:		*Price band (£)*
	Full rod (1 agreed day per week, 4 fish per day)	255.00–290.00
	Half rod (1 agreed day per fortnight, 4 fish per day)	137.00–165.00
	Day ticket (4 fish)	11.50–14.00
	Evening ticket (2 fish)	6.00–7.50

Young person may share rod with accompanying adult
Additional day tickets for members only (2 fish: £7.00).

BOATS:	Boats available. Maximum 2 anglers per boat. 50p basic charge + 50p per $3\frac{1}{2}$ hour period.
STOCKING POLICY:	Stocking daily. Rainbows and browns.
PERMITS:	Reservations required, not more than seven days in advance. Evening tickets up to 30 days in advance. Thames Water Authority licence required, available at lodge.
GENERAL INFORMATION:	9,313 fish taken by 4,006 rods. Average weight: 2 lb 2 oz. 3,826 fish taken between 2 lb and 3 lb. Maximum hook size: 1 in. No. 8. Overall fly: $1\frac{1}{4}$ in.

LEIGHTON RESERVOIR
Healey, Masham, Ripon, North Yorkshire
Tel: Masham (076 582) 224 or 713

Location: 4 miles west of Masham

THE WATER:	113 acres. Fishing hut.	
SEASON:	Latter part of April to mid-October.	
HOURS:	Dawn until dusk (but not later than 10.30 p.m.)	
COSTS:	Full rod (6 fish per day) Day ticket (6 fish)	*Price band (£)* 110.00–125.00 5.00–6.00
	Children under 14 and disabled persons half-price.	
STOCKING POLICY:	Stocking weekly, to maintain average catch rate 2.4 fish per rod per day. Rainbows ranging from $\frac{3}{4}$ lb to 4 lb. Some browns.	
PERMITS:	Reservations not required. Put money in envelope and place in safe deposit box. Yorkshire Water Authority licence required, obtainable from F. A. Plumpton (Hairdresser), Silver Street, Masham, Ripon, North Yorkshire.	
GENERAL INFORMATION:	Recommended flies are Sedges, Black Gnats, Black and Peacock, Baby Doll and Muddlers. The area of the dam wall seems to catch most fish.	

LEOMINSTEAD TROUT FISHERY
Emery Down, Lyndhurst, Hampshire
Tel: Lyndhurst (042 128) 2610

Location: Near Lyndhurst, near A35, near A337

THE WATER:	8 acres. Fishing hut, WC. Flies available on premises. Tackle may be hired. Maximum number of rods per day: 26.	
SEASON:	Beginning April to end October.	
HOURS:	9.00 a.m. to sunset.	
COSTS:		*Price band (£)*
	Full rod (30 weeks, 1 day per week, 4 fish)	270.00–305.00
	Half rod (15 weeks, 1 day per fortnight, 4 fish)	144.00–170.00
	Day ticket (4 fish)	10.50–12.00
	Half-day ticket (2 fish)	6.00–7.00
	All prices include VAT	
	Additional day tickets available, 8 fish maximum	
STOCKING POLICY:	Main stocking before beginning of season. Topped up regularly throughout. Rainbow trout 1½ lb upwards, average weight 2½ lb.	
PERMITS:	Booking advisable, by phone or letter. Fishermen to call at office at the lakeside before commencing fishing. Southern Water Authority licence required, available from Fishery Office.	
GENERAL INFORMATION:	Lakeside caravan available for weekly letting. Average catch 3 fish per rod. Recomended flies & lures	

April, May: Jack Frost, Zulu, Baby Doll, Marabou, Dambuster, Black & Silver.
June, July, August: Damsel Nymphs, Black Buzzers, Orange Nymphs, Whisky, Muddlers, White Marabou, Black and Peacock, Black Spider, Coachman.
September: Daddy Long Legs, Sedge, Orange Nymph, Dambuster.
October: White/black Marabou, Black and Silver, Zulu, Orange Nymph, Dambuster.

Leominstead is a natural stream-fed lake, enlarged and deepened 300 years ago. Landing stages on three banks to facilitate casting. The fourth bank has a grassed 'beach' to the water.

There are no particular 'hot spots' where the fish gather. The lake is 25 ft deep in places but the fish are never usually that deep. Experience has shown that it is far better to stay on one landing stage, or spot, rather than change position too frequently as after a while the fish will 'come' to the angler. It is recommended that the angler casts alongside the bank, near to the bushes, and fishes two or three feet below the surface.

LINACRE RESERVOIR
Cutthorpe, near Chesterfield, Derbyshire
c/o STWA Office, Dimple Road, Matlock, Derbyshire
Tel: Matlock (0629) 55051

Location: 2 miles north-west of Chesterfield. Near B6050

THE WATER:	Three reservoirs totalling 44 acres. No lodge facilities. Maximum number of rods per day: 20.	
SEASON:	1 April to 30 September (1 to 7 April full rods only).	
HOURS:	One hour before sunrise to one hour after sunset.	
COSTS:		*Price band (£)*
	Full rod (4 fish per day)	69.00–85.00
	Day ticket High Season (4 fish)	4.00–5.50
	Day ticket Low Season (4 fish)	3.60–5.50
	Concessionary ticket (2 fish)	2.00–2.75

Concessionary permits available for children under 16, disabled, OAP.
Permits available from: Mr. F. Hall, 9 Beetwell St, Chesterfield. Tel: (0246) 73133.
Advanced booking and permits from Fishery Office, Linacre Reservoir (weekends 10.00 a.m. to 4.00 p.m. only), or STWA Office (address above).

STOCKING POLICY: 2,850 browns, 1,750 rainbows. Stocked at approximately fortnightly intervals.

PERMITS: Yorkshire Water Authority licence required. Reservations not required, but limited number of day permits available.

GENERAL INFORMATION: 2,354 fish taken by 1,069 rods.

LINCH HILL: STONEACRES
Linch Hill Fishery, Stanton Harcourt, Oxon
Tel: Oxford (0865) 882 215

Location: Off the B4449, approximately half-way between Stanton Harcourt and Standlake in Oxfordshire

THE WATER:	58 acres. Lodge facilities. Telephone and drinks machine. Flies sold, tackle hire. Fish smoked for anglers. Maximum number of rods per day: 120.
SEASON:	Mid-March to 31 October: season and day tickets. 1 November to 3 January: day tickets. Winter season available.
HOURS:	Season tickets: 6.00 a.m. to 1 hour after sunset Day tickets: 9.00 a.m. to 1 hour after sunset

COSTS:		Price band (£)
	Full rod (8 fish per week)	120.00–140.00
	Mid-week full rod (4 fish per week)	80.00–95.00
	Day ticket (5 fish)	8.00–10.00
	Evening ticket (3 fish)	5.50–6.50

	Half-price for Junior tickets (under 16 years of age). Additional day tickets available, same price as above. Above prices include VAT. Undamaged fish can be returned, but once bag has been killed another ticket must be purchased.
BOATS:	Six boats available. 1 or 2 fishermen per boat. Reservations required. Anchors provided. Costs: £5.00–6.00 per day. £3.00–4.00 evening.
STOCKING POLICY:	Stocking weekly and more often if required. 100 fish per acre. 12 oz +, also larger fish. Average: 1½ lb. Mainly rainbow, record 10 lb.
PERMITS:	Reservations not required. Tickets issued at reception. Thames Water Authority licence required, available on site.
GENERAL INFORMATION:	Average catch: 2.5 fish per visit. 12,500 fish caught during season. Special facilities for disabled: casting platform, WC, in good weather can take cars around the bank. Economy holiday tickets and party concessions. Overnight vans (but not caravans) allowed. All flies to be tied on single hooks not exceeding size No. 6. All fish taken must exceed 12 in. for rainbows and 14 in for browns. Undersized fish must be returned alive to the water.

Good mayfly hatches in June. Good sedge hatches late July–October. Early season: black lure, Viva, Muddler. July–November: Green and Amber Nymph.

LINCH HILL: WILLOW POOL
Linch Hill Fishery, Stanton Harcourt, Oxon.
Tel: Oxford (0865) 882 215

Location: Off the B4449, approximately half-way between Stanton Harcourt and Standlake in Oxfordshire

THE WATER:	10 acres. Willow Pool has own lodge. Main lodge contains telephone, drinks machine. Flies sold, tackle hire. Fish smoked for anglers. Maximum number of rods per day: 10 on bank and 4 in boats.
SEASON:	Mid-March to 31 October: season and day tickets. 1 November to 3 January: day tickets.
HOURS:	Season tickets: 6.00 a.m. to 1 hour after sunset Day tickets: 9.00 a.m. to 1 hour after sunset.
COSTS:	*Price band (£)* Full rod (1 named weekend day, 4 fish) 400.00–450.00 Full rod (one named weekday, 4 fish) 260.00–300.00 Day ticket (5 fish) 20.00–23.00 Evening ticket (3 fish) 13.00–16.00 Half-price for Junior tickets (under 16 years of age) Additional day tickets available, same price as above. *All prices include VAT*
BOATS:	Two boats available. 1 or 2 fishermen per boat. Reservations required. Anchors provided. Costs: £7.50–8.50 per day £5.00–6.00 half day.
STOCKING POLICY:	100 fish per acre. Minimum $1\frac{1}{2}$ lb. Average 4 lb. Mainly rainbows. Stocking on put and take basis, usually daily. Record 14 lb 11 oz, with many double-figure fish caught.
PERMITS:	Reservations advisable. Tickets issued at reception. Thames Water Authority licence required, available on site.

GENERAL INFORMATION:	Exclusive block booking possible: 10 rods maximum at £180.00–210.00 per day.
	  Average catch: 3 fish per rod. Average bag: 12 lb.
	  All flies to be tied on single hooks not exceeding size No. 6. All fish taken must exceed 12 in. for rainbows and 14 in. for browns. All fish must be killed.
	  Willow Pool is fairly sheltered and not much affected by wind. Larger fish are generally caught on lures lower down. Dog fly is popular June–November. Good hatches of mayfly and sedge.

LINFORD LAKES
c/o Linch Hill Fishery, Stanton Harcourt, Oxon.
Tel: Oxford (0865) 882 215

Location: Newport Pagnell, Bucks. Close to the M1 and may be reached via the A422

THE WATER:	Three lakes totalling 30 acres. Small hut for registration. Maximum number of rods per day: 60. Season only.
SEASON:	Mid-March to 31 October.
HOURS:	6.00 a.m. to 1 hour after sunset.
COSTS:	Full rod (8 fish per week) *Price band (£)* 120.00–140.00 Mid-week full rod (4 fish per week) 80.00–95.00 Undamaged fish can be returned.
STOCKING POLICY:	Stocking twice monthly or more often if required. 100 fish per acre. 12 oz + with some bigger fish. Rainbows.
PERMITS:	Club hut for registration on arrival and departure. Anglian Water Authority licence required.
GENERAL INFORMATION:	Average: 50 fish per full rod. Lure fishing is preferred at beginning and end of season. Good hatches of sedge, buzzers from June to October. All flies to be tied on single hooks not exceeding size No. 6. All rainbows must exceed 12 in.

LITTLE HEATH FARM
Little Heath Road, Gamlingay, Sandy, Bedfordshire
Tel: Sandy (0767) 50310

Location: Off B1042, off B1040

THE WATER:	6 acres. Maximum number of rods per day: 10.	
SEASON:	Early April to end October.	
HOURS:	7.30 a.m. to dusk.	
		Price band (£)
COSTS:	Day ticket (4 fish)	7.50–9.00
	Half-day ticket (2 fish)	3.75–4.75
BOATS:	£1.50–2.00 per angler.	
PERMITS:	Reservations required.	

LOCKINGE FISHERY
Lockinge, Wantage, Oxon
Estate Office – Tel: East Hendred (023 588) 200
Water keeper – Tel: East Hendred (023 588) 239

Location: Approximately $2\frac{1}{2}$ miles east of Wantage

THE WATER:	Season only. Lockinge Lake: 3.7 acres. Ardington Lake: 1.9 acres. Fishing hut. Water keeper runs village shop 100 yards from hut. Maximum number: 40 season rods per year.	
SEASON:	1 April to 30 September.	
HOURS:	To one hour after sunset.	
COSTS:	Full rod (5 fish per week)	*Price band (£)* 265–300 + VAT
	No additional day tickets available.	
STOCKING POLICY:	Stocking as and when necessary.	
PERMITS:	Reservations required. Season rods only. Thames Valley Water Board licence required, available on premises.	
GENERAL INFORMATION:	2,218 fish taken by 38 members. Single flies only, on single hook, wet, dry or nymph, on hook not larger than size No. 10.	

LOCKWOOD BECK RESERVOIR
Cleveland
c/o Northumbrian Water Authority, Tees Division, Trenchard Avenue, Thornaby, Stockton, Cleveland
Tel: Stockton (0642) 62216

Location: Close to the A171 — Guisborough to Whitby Road

THE WATER:	60 acres. Altitude 615 ft. Lodge facilities. WC. No limit to number of rods per day.	
SEASON:	1 April to 30 September.	
HOURS:	6.00 a.m. to 7.00 p.m.	
		Price band (£)
COSTS:	Full rod (8 fish 9 in. minimum size)	100.00+
	OAP, disabled and children under 16	50.00+
	Day ticket (8 fish, 9 in. minimum size)	4.00+
	OAP, disabled and children under 16	2.00+
	Weekly ticket	16.00+
	OAP, disabled and children under 16	8.00+
BOATS:	Boats available from 8.30 a.m. for two anglers. May be reserved. Costs: £5.00+ per day £3.00+ per evening.	
STOCKING POLICY:	Browns only.	
PERMITS:	No reservations required. Self-service facilities for day tickets. Northumbrian Water Authority licence required, Contact Tees Division (address above).	
GENERAL INFORMATION:	Fly only. 4,417 fish taken by 3,541 (recorded) rods.	

LOWER MOOR FISHERY
Oaksey, Malmesbury, Wiltshire
Tel: Minety (066 640) 232

Location: Near Oaksey, near Malmesbury

THE WATER:	Mallard Lake: 30 acres. Cottage Lake: 8 acres. Swallow Pool: 7 acres. Lodge. WC. Calor gas stove for making tea or coffee. Food available for group booking, by prior arrangement. Maximum number of rods per day: 50.
SEASON:	Late March to end of October.
HOURS:	8.00 a.m. to sunset.
COSTS:	*Price band (£)* Day ticket (4 fish) 8.50–9.50 Season, half-rods, junior and evening tickets available. Junior and evening tickets: 2 fish. Additional day tickets available. Price as above.
STOCKING POLICY:	Stocking usually weekly. 80–100 fish per acre. Rainbows: $1\frac{1}{4}$ lb to 4 lb Browns: 1 lb to 3 lb Swallow Pool: 90% browns Mallard Lake and Cottage Lake: 75% rainbows, 25% browns and American brooks.
PERMITS:	Reservations recommended. Self-service facilities available at office. Thames Water Authority licence required, available on premises.
GENERAL INFORMATION:	'Teach-ins' for junior and inexperienced adults. Individual tuition can be arranged. 9,237 fish taken. Average: 2.64 fish per rod visit. Cottage Lake and Swallow Pool are restricted to nymph or dry fly only on a floating line. Clear water. Abundance of fly life. Prolific Mayfly hatch, usually lasts 6–8 weeks. Pheasant Tail and Mayfly Nymphs most productive. One fly only on cast. Group bookings can be arranged.

MALHAM TARN FIELD CENTRE
near Settle, North Yorks
Tel: Airton (07293) 331

Location: From the North – leave the M6 at exit 36 and follow the A65 to Settle. From the South – leave the M6 at exit 31 and follow A59 to Gisburn. In village take the left turn signposted to Settle. From Settle – from the A65 turn left immediately after the bridge on B6479. From A59 come through Settle, pass under two railway bridges; after second bridge proceed $\frac{1}{4}$ mile and turn right just before bridge on to B6479. Proceed one mile, then take small turning to right into Langcliffe village (signposted Malham). Follow road up over moors; at top of long hill turn right at T junction. Take left fork at next Y junction. Follow on for about $1-1\frac{1}{2}$ miles until sharp left bend signposted Arncliffe. Turn right on untarred road with National Trust signposts. Centre is about $\frac{1}{2}$ mile along road

THE WATER:	153 acres. Maximum number of rods per day: 12.
SEASON:	1 May to 30 September.
HOURS:	Mondays to Fridays: 9.00 a.m.–7.30 p.m. Saturdays: 9.00 a.m.–9.00 p.m. or sunset (whichever is earlier) Sundays: 10.00 a.m.–9.00 p.m. or sunset (whichever is earlier)
COSTS:	Price band (£) Day ticket (6 fish) 3.50–4.75 All prices include VAT Reduced prices for young people.
BOATS:	Four boats available. 1–3 fishermen per boat. Reservations recommended. No anchors provided. Costs: Monday to Friday – £4.50–6.00. Saturday and Sunday – £5.75–7.00.
STOCKING POLICY:	2,000 trout are put into the Tarn early in each year: 1,500 at 4 in. to 5 in. and 500 at 9 in. to 11 in.
PERMITS:	Yorkshire Water Authority licence required. May be purchased from Field Centre Office. Reservations required.
GENERAL INFORMATION:	Hire of fishing rod: £2.00–2.50 per day. (Two available). Size limit of trout: 11 in. The Tarn can be very rough. It is situated at 1,250 ft on the Pennines in open moorland. Until the end of June fishermen are asked to avoid the north-west corner because of nesting birds (estate is a bird sanctuary). Life jackets available in Field Centre office. Warm clothing is vital. Unaccompanied children under 16 not advised because of weather conditions. (Sometimes three adult men cannot get the boat back to the boathouse.)

Anglers may use Field Centre as a residential base for fishing in the Tarn at any time during fishing season. Charge is £95.00–110.00 per week, including full use of boats, board and lodging. Enquiries to The Warden.

MARTINS TROUT LAKE
Martin's Farm, Woodlands, Wimborne, Dorset
Tel: Verwood (0202) 822335

Location: Approximately 15 miles from Bournemouth

THE WATER:	$2\frac{1}{2}$ acres. No lodge facilities. Maximum number of rods per day: 6.	
SEASON:	1 April to 31 October.	
HOURS:	8.30 a.m. to one hour past sunset.	
		Price band (£)
COSTS:	Day ticket (3 fish)	£7.50–9.00
	Half-day ticket (2 fish)	5.50–6.50
	All prices include VAT	
BOATS:	Two boats available. £1.00–2.00 per hour.	
STOCKING POLICY:	All rainbows. Stocking weekly to replace fish caught.	
PERMITS:	Reservations advisable. No water authority licence required.	
GENERAL INFORMATION:	Fish from $\frac{3}{4}$ lb to $2\frac{1}{2}$–3 lb. Caravan Club registered facilities.	

MILL FARM FISHERY
Mill Farm, Peatling Parva Road, Gilmorton, Lutterworth, Leicestershire.
Tel: Lutterworth (045 55) 2392

Location: Off Junction 20 M1/A50/A427

THE WATER:	$3\frac{1}{2}$ acres.	
SEASON:	Mid-March to mid-June.	
HOURS:	Dawn to one hour after sunset.	
		Price band (£)
COSTS:	Day ticket	4.00–5.25
	Evening ticket	2.00–2.75
BOATS:	One to two anglers.	
	Cost: £2.00–2.75	

MOREHALL RESERVOIR
c/o Yorkshire Water Authority, West Riding House, Albion Street, Leeds
Tel: Leeds (0532) 448201

Location: In Ewden Valley, near Stocksbridge, South Yorkshire. 9 miles north-west of Sheffield. Route via A616

THE WATER:	65 acres. No lodge facilities. Chemical WCs situated around reservoir. No limit to number of rods.	
SEASON:	25 March to 30 September.	
HOURS:	7.00 a.m. to dusk.	
COSTS:	Day ticket (2 fish, 11 in. minimum size)	*Price band (£)* 1.50–2.25
	A limited number of season permits available, particulars from address below. No additional day tickets available.	
STOCKING POLICY:	Stocking with browns and rainbows before the commencement of season, then monthly throughout the season.	
PERMITS:	No reservations required. Day tickets sold by ticket-dispensing machines at reservoir. No half-day tickets available. Yorkshire Water Authority licence required by all anglers 10 and above, not sold at reservoir.	
GENERAL INFORMATION:	Fly only. Season permits information: Public Relations Officer, Yorkshire Water Authority, Castle Market Building, Exchange Street, Sheffield (Tel: Sheffield (0742) 26421 Ext. 16).	

NEWELLS LAKE FISHERIES
near Horsham, West Sussex
Tel: Southwater (0403) 730 505

Location: Near A24, near A264. Near Horsham

THE WATER:	5 acres.	
SEASON:	Beginning April to end September.	

		Price band (£)
COSTS:	Full rod (weekend)	170.00–195.00
	Full rod (weekdays)	140.00–165.00
	Day ticket (mid-week, 4 fish)	8.50–10.50
	Day ticket (weekend, 4 fish)	10.00–12.00
	Evening ticket (2 fish)	5.00–6.50
BOATS:	Boats available.	
PERMITS:	Reservations required. Suggested one week in advance.	

OGSTON RESERVOIR
Alfreton, near Chesterfield, Derbyshire
c/o STWA Office, 43 Dimple Road, Matlock, Derbyshire
Tel: Matlock (0629) 55051

Location: Near Clay Cross. Adjacent to B6014. 10 miles south of Chesterfield

THE WATER:	203 acres. No lodge facilities. Maximum number of rods per day: 15.
SEASON:	1 April to mid-October.
HOURS:	One hour before sunrise to one hour after sunset.

COSTS:		*Price band (£)*
	Day ticket High Season (2 fish)	3.40–4.50
	Day ticket Low Season (2 fish)	3.10–4.25
	Concessionary day ticket (1 fish)	1.70–2.25

	Concessionary permits available for children under 16, disabled, OAP. Advanced booking and permits available from STWA office (address above) or New Napoleon Inn, Woolley Moor, near Ogston Reservoir. Tel: 0246 590413.
STOCKING POLICY:	4,250 browns and rainbows.
PERMITS:	Severn Trent Water Authority licence required. Reservations recommended. 15 day permits only.
GENERAL INFORMATION:	295 fish caught by 435 rods. Rainbows may not be taken before 16 May.

OTTERHEAD RESERVOIR
Taunton, Somerset
c/o Wessex Water Authority, P.O. Box 9, King Square, Bridgwater
Tel: (027) 57333

Location: On the Blackdown Hills south of Taunton, 1 mile north of the village of Churchingford

THE WATER:	Two lakes of 2 acres each. Lodge facilities. WC. No limit to number of rods per day.	
SEASON:	Beginning April to mid-October.	
HOURS:	8.00 a.m. until one hour after sunset.	
COSTS:		*Price band (£)*
	Full rod	55.00–70.00
	Day tickets (6 fish)	4.50–6.00
	Junior, OAP approximately half price. Full rod permits available from Divisional Fisheries and Recreations Officer, Somerset Division (address above).	
STOCKING POLICY:	Stocking every 8–14 days. Usually 200 fish per acre. Size range: $1\frac{1}{4}$ lb to 2 lb. 75% rainbows, 25% browns.	
PERMITS:	No reservations required. Self-service kiosks for day tickets. No water authority licence required.	
GENERAL INFORMATION:	30,000 fish stocked in total Wessex Water Authority reservoir area of 389 acres. 17,000 fish taken, from $1\frac{1}{2}$ lb to 4 lb.	

OUGHTON TROUT FISHERY
Burford Ray Lodge, Bedford Road, Hitchin, Herts
Tel: Hitchin (0462) 4201

Location: Off A600 − 2 miles north of Hitchin, close to Turnpike Lane

THE WATER:	$2\frac{3}{4}$ acres. Maximum number of rods per day: 10.	
SEASON:	Beginning March to end October.	
HOURS:	9.00 a.m. to dark.	
		Price band (£)
COSTS:	Full rod	160.00–195.00
	Half rod	80.00–100.00
	Day ticket (5 fish)	6.90–8.25
	Half day (3 fish)	4.90–6.25
STOCKING POLICY:	150 fish per acre.	
PERMITS:	Reservations strongly recommended. Thames Water Authority licence required.	
GENERAL INFORMATION:	Almost 3,000 fish taken during season. Average about 2.5 per rod.	

OVERWATER LAKE
Ireby, Carlisle, Cumbria
Tel: Aspatria (0965) 20010

Location: Near Carlisle, near Penrith

THE WATER:	$29\frac{1}{2}$ acres. Maximum number of rods per day: 30–40.	
SEASON:	No close season for rainbows.	
HOURS:	6.00 a.m. until sunset.	
COSTS:	Day ticket (4 fish)	*Price band (£)* 5.00–5.50
	Additional day tickets: £5.00–5.50. Tickets available from: D. W. Lothian, Fishing Tackle Shop, Cockermouth or Mr. Warwick, White Field Cottage, Ireby, Carlisle.	
BOATS:	Two boats available, issued on first come, first served basis. No anchors provided. Cost: £4.00–4.50 per person per day. (£10.00 deposit required.)	
STOCKING POLICY:	Lake stocked with 70 fish per acre and thereafter once per month with 4 fish for every permit sold during the previous month. Size range: 10 oz to 8–10 lb.	
PERMITS:	North West Water Authority licence required, can be obtained from D. W. Lothian, Fishing Tackle Shop, Cockermouth.	
GENERAL INFORMATION:	Regulations in accordance with the by-laws of North West Water Authority.	

PACKINGTON FISHERIES
Fishery Lodge, Broadwater, Maxstoke Lane, Meriden, near Coventry, West Midlands
Tel: Meriden (0676) 22754

Location: Off Maxstoke Lane near Meriden, near Coventry

THE WATER:	Three lakes totalling 35 acres available on day ticket. Three other lakes totalling 52 acres, members only. Flies and limited selection of tackle available from the fishery office. Clubhouse offering bar, snack and restaurant facilities seven days a week. Maximum number of day tickets: 90. Maximum members on separate waters: 36.
SEASON:	Mid-March to mid-November.
HOURS:	6.00 a.m. to one hour after sunset.

COSTS:

	Price band (£)
Full rod (34 weeks, 1 named day)	230.00–260.00 + VAT
Half rod (17 fortnightly visits, 1 named day)	125.00–145.00 + VAT
Day ticket	7.00–8.00 (incl. VAT)
Evening ticket (from 2.30 p.m.)	4.50–5.00 (incl. VAT)
Junior tickets (under 16 years) day	4.00–4.50 (incl. VAT)
Junior tickets (under 16 years) evening	3.00–3.50 (incl. VAT)

No bag limits.

BOATS:	Boats available. 1 or 2 persons per boat. Costs: £3.00–3.50 per boat (incl. VAT) per day. £2.00–2.50 per boat (incl. VAT) per evening. Boats available before 8.00 a.m. where they have been pre-booked.
STOCKING POLICY:	Stocking on a regular weekly put and take basis, with browns and rainbows from 12 in. upwards. Total catch: 27,000.
PERMITS:	Telephone bookings for day tickets are acceptable, but are only confirmed by receipt of fees. Self-service before 8.00 a.m. Severn-Trent Water Authority Licence required.
GENERAL INFORMATION:	Average fish per rod visit: 1.9. Basic lure fishing is most productive early season, with black lures and slow sinking lines. May – good hatches small buzzer, Alder, Hawthorn; mid-morning and early afternoon: use Black, Green, Olive Nymphs, Greenwells, Wickhams, Invicta and Amber Nymphs. June – teams of mixed flies most successful. July – sedge activity, Stick Fly

Caddis, Amber Nymphs, Muddler, Damsel Nymph. August – a sunken line, using lures – Jersey Herd, Dog Nobbler. September – Butcher, Dunkeld, Black Pennell. October – Buzzers and Nymphs alternating with lures. November – mainly lures on sinking lines.

Maximum hook size: No. 8. Maximum size of fly: $1\frac{1}{2}$ in.

PATSHULL PARK FISHERY
Temple Hotel, Patshull Park, Burnhill Green, Wolverhampton, Staffordshire
Tel: Pattingham (0902) 700100

Location: Near A454, near A464. Entrance near Pattingham, near Wolverhampton

THE WATER:	86 acres. Lodge facilities. Flies and tackle available. Snacks in Sportsman Bar. Restaurant. Maximum number of rods per day: 300.
SEASON:	Open all year round except Christmas Day.
HOURS:	7.30 a.m. to dusk.

		Price band (£)
COSTS:	Day ticket	9.50–10.50
	Half-day ticket	4.75–5.50
	Books of ten tickets	85.00–100.00
	Above prices include VAT	

No bag limit on Great Pool.

BOATS:	Thirty boats available, seats 3. Anchors provided. Costs: £4.00–5.00 per day £2.50–3.00 per half day.
STOCKING POLICY:	Stocking daily with rainbows. All fish caught are replaced.
PERMITS:	Reservations not required, but are advisable for fishermen requiring boats. Tickets available from Temple Hotel Reception. Severn-Trent Waterboard Licence required, available on premises.
GENERAL INFORMATION:	Average fish per rod: 3.1. Most successful fishing methods with regard to flies, month by month: January to March: Slow sink lines. Lures, Black and Yellow Dog Nobblers. April to June: Lures deep fished, Damsel Nymph, Walkers Mayfly Nymph and Pheasant Tail. July to September: Buzzers and Nymphs. October to December: Damsel Nymphs, Fry and Lures. Accommodation available at hotel on premises.

PEATSWOOD LAKES
Market Drayton, Shropshire
Reservations: Broomhall Lodge, Peatswood, Market Drayton, Salopshire
Tel: Market Drayton (0630) 4505

Location: Off Berrisford Road

THE WATER:	Two lakes of 2 acres and 5 acres.	
SEASON:	Mid-March to mid-November.	
HOURS:	9.00 a.m. to dusk.	
		Price band (£)
COSTS:	Full rod	125.00–175.00
	Day ticket (4 fish)	7.00–9.00
	No additional day tickets available.	
PERMITS:	Reservations strongly recommended.	
GENERAL INFORMATION:	Almost 4,000 fish landed during season.	

PECKHAM'S COPSE
North Mundham, Chichester, Sussex
Southern Leisure Centre, Chichester
Tel: Chichester (0243) 787 715

Location: Off B2166. Approximately 2 miles south-east of Chichester

THE WATER:	Two lakes of 20 acres each.	
SEASON:	Beginning April to end October.	
COSTS:	Day ticket (4 fish)	*Price band (£)* 10.50–12.00
BOATS:	Boats available.	
STOCKING POLICY:	200 fish per acre in 2 lb range.	
PERMITS:	Reservations strongly recommended.	

PITSFORD RESERVOIR
Pitsford, near Northampton, Northamptonshire
Tel: Walgrave St. Peters (060 126) 350

Location: Near Northampton/Kettering. Near A508

THE WATER:	739 acres. Lodge facilities. WC. No limit to number of rods per day.	
SEASON:	1 April to 29 October.	
HOURS:	One hour before sunrise to one hour after sunset.	
COSTS:		*Price band (£)*
	Full rod (8 fish per day)	75.00–90.00
	Day ticket (8 fish)	3.00–3.50
	Juniors	1.50–1.80
	Evening ticket (after 5.00 p.m. May–August, after 4.00 p.m. April and September)	2.00–2.50
	No additional day tickets available.	
BOATS:	Twelve boats, 2 persons per boat. Anchors provided. Costs: £3.30–4.00 per day £1.90–2.30 per evening.	
STOCKING POLICY:	22,500 trout per season. 90% rainbows, 10% brown. Average size: 12 in.	
PERMITS:	Reservations required for boat fishing. Welland and Nene River Division rod licence required, available at reservoir.	
GENERAL INFORMATION:	1.97 fish per rod (based on returned forms). Anglian Water Authority (Northampton Water Division) Northampton (0604) 21321.	

POOH CORNER
Rolvenden, Cranbrook, Kent
Tel: Rolvenden (058 084) 219

Location: Off B2086/A28

THE WATER:	Two pools of approximately 2 acres each. Lodge facilities for making tea and coffee. Flies and tackle available in lodge. Maximum number of rods per day: 8.
SEASON:	Beginning April to end October.
HOURS:	8.30 a.m. to one hour after sunset.

		Price band (£)
COSTS:	Day ticket (4 fish)	9.00–10.50
	Evening ticket (after 4.00 p.m., 2 fish)	4.50–5.75

Additional day tickets available same price as above.

STOCKING POLICY:	Rainbows and browns stocked daily. Minimum weight: 1 lb. Fish up to 3 lb present.
PERMITS:	Reservations advisable, at least a week in advance. No local water authority licence required.
GENERAL INFORMATION:	Fly-casting instruction available. One fly only. Conventional flies to be used. Large lures banned. Pools vary in depth from 3 ft to 18 ft.

PORTH RESERVOIR
near Newquay, Cornwall
Tel: Newquay (063 73) 2701

Location: Off A3059 near A39/A392

THE WATER:	40 acres. No lodge facilities. No limit to number of rods.	
SEASON:	1 April to 31 October.	
HOURS:	One hour before sunrise to one hour after sunset.	
		Price band (£)
COSTS:	Day ticket (5 fish)	4.50–6.00
	OAP, disabled, student under 18, junior under 16	3.50–5.00
	Child under 14	1.00–1.50
	Evening (after 4.00 p.m., 3 fish)	2.50–3.50
	Book of 20 permits available at 15% discount. No additional day tickets available.	
BOATS:	Pulling boats available, seats 2. Anchors provided. No boats Tuesdays or Wednesdays. No boats after 12 October. Costs: £4.50–5.50 per day. £3.00–3.50 half day (after 4.00 p.m.) Telephone Warden to book.	
STOCKING POLICY:	Pre-season stocking of browns and rainbows, then trickle stocking throughout the season with fish averaging over 1 lb.	
PERMITS:	No reservations required. Tickets on self-service, no change available. No local water authority licence required.	
GENERAL INFORMATION:	3,105 fish caught during season. 1.7 fish per rod day. Small green or black flies do well during most of the season, particularly when water warms up. Lures are successful early season but effectiveness reduces after the first month or so.	
	South West Water Authority.	

POWDERMILL RESERVOIR
near Sedlescombe, East Sussex
Tel: Sedlescombe (042 487) 248
Hastings Flyfishers Club Ltd., 3 Endwell Road, Bexhill-on-Sea.

Location: Off A229 Maidstone to Hastings Road, then left on to Brede Road

THE WATER:	55 acres.	
SEASON:	Beginning May to end October.	
HOURS:	9.00 a.m. to one hour past sunset.	
		Price band (£)
COSTS:	Day ticket (6 fish)	7.50–9.00
BOATS:	1 to 2 rods. Costs: £3.00–4.00 per day.	
PERMITS:	Reservations recommended. Southern Water Authority licence required.	

RAVENSTHORPE RESERVOIR
Ravensthorpe, near Northampton, Northamptonshire
Tel: East Haddon (060 125) 210

Location: Off A50, near M1. Near Northampton

THE WATER:	114 acres. No limit to number of rods per day.	
SEASON:	1 April to 29 October.	
HOURS:	One hour before sunrise to one hour after sunset.	
COSTS:		*Price band (£)*
	Full rod (8 fish per day)	75.00–90.00
	Day tickets (8 fish)	3.00–3.50
	Juniors	1.50–1.80
	Evening ticket (after 5.00 p.m. May–August, after 4.00 p.m. April and September)	2.00–2.50
	No additional day tickets available.	
BOATS:	Eight boats, 2 persons per boat. Anchors provided. Costs: £3.30–4.00 per day. £1.90–2.30 per evening.	
STOCKING POLICY:	7,500 trout per season. 90% rainbows, 10% browns. Average size: 12 in.	
PERMITS:	Reservations required for boat fishing. Welland and Nene River Division rod licence required, available at reservoir.	
GENERAL INFORMATION:	1.97 fish per rod (based on returned forms). Anglian Water Authority (Northampton Water Division) Northampton (0604) 21321.	

RINGSTEAD GRANGE TROUT FISHERY
Ringstead, Kettering, Northants
Tel: Wellingborough (0933) 622960

Location: 3 miles off A6. 7 miles Kettering. 7 miles Wellingborough. 3 miles Thrapston. 5 miles Rushden.
Lake is off Ringstead to Great Addington Road. 1 mile from Ringstead

THE WATER:	36 acres. Lodge. Gas stove. Kettle, teapot, tea, sugar, milk, plastic cups free. Maximum number of rods per day: 30 bank plus boat anglers.
SEASON:	Early April to end October.
HOURS:	7.00 a.m. to one hour after sunset.

COSTS:		Price band (£)
	Day ticket (6 fish)	4.00–4.50
	Evening ticket (after 5.00 p.m., 3 fish)	2.50–2.75

No additional day tickets available. Two evening tickets allowed. Fish may be returned to water.

BOATS:	Six boats available for one or two anglers. Reservations recommended. Anchors and oars provided. Costs: £6.00–7.50 per day £3.00–3.75 per evening.
STOCKING POLICY:	Regular stocking policy with rainbows, browns and brooks (12 in. minimum).
PERMITS:	Reservations required first fortnight of season. Afterwards recommended. Nene and Welland rod licence (Anglian Water Authority) required, available on premises.
GENERAL INFORMATION:	Average: 2.3 fish per rod. Best limit bag: 22 lb 15 oz.

R.O.K. POOL TROUT FISHERY
near Ipswich, Suffolk
Tel: King's Langley (09277) 65772

Location: North of Ipswich, near Stowmarket, near A45

THE WATER:	$4\frac{1}{2}$ acres. Lodge. Season only unless staying at cottage. Maximum number of rods per day: 7.	
SEASON:	Beginning April to end September.	
HOURS:	9.00 a.m. to dark.	
		Price band (£)
COSTS:	Full rod (1 named day per week, 4 fish)	155.00–180.00
	Half rod (1 named day per fortnight, 4 fish)	85.00–105.00
STOCKING POLICY:	Range 1 lb to 7 lb. Stocked daily. Average size: 2 lb. 100+ fish per acre. 50% rainbows, 40% brooks, 10% browns.	
PERMITS:	Reservations required. Anglian Water Authority licence required, not available on site.	
GENERAL INFORMATION:	Dry fly nymph water only. Two droppers permitted. Maximum hook size No. 10 long shank. Cottages available to let by week, price including one or two rods.	

ROOKSBURY MILL TROUT FISHERY
Rooksbury Road, Andover, Hants
Tel: Andover (0264) 52921

Location: Near A303, near A3057. Andover

THE WATER:	Two lakes, 3 acres and 7 acres. Lodge, tackle shop.	
SEASON:	Beginning April to end October.	
COSTS:		*Price band (£)*
	Full rod	253.00–290.00
	Half rod	126.50–145.00
	Ten weekdays	95.00–110.00
	Day ticket (5 fish)	12.00–14.00
	Half-day ticket	6.00–7.00
STOCKING POLICY:	Stocked weekly with rainbows and browns.	
PERMITS:	Reservations recommended.	
GENERAL INFORMATION:	Average weight: $2\frac{1}{4}$ lb. Average catch per day: 2.5 fish. One mile of bank on River Anton available for stocked browns.	

RUSHMOOR TROUT LAKES
Upper Lodge, Henley Common, Fernhurst, Haslemere, Surrey
Tel: Haslemere (0428) 2818

Location: Rushmoor, near Hindhead, Surrey

THE WATER:	Three small lakes. Fishing hut.
SEASON:	Beginning April to end September.
HOURS:	9.00 a.m. to one hour after sunset.

Price band (£)

COSTS:	Day ticket (4 fish)	10.00–11.50
	All prices include VAT	
PERMITS:	Thames Water Authority licence required. Reservations required.	
GENERAL INFORMATION:	Fishing may continue after limit has been taken, with barbless hooks.	

RUTLAND WATER
Empingham, Oakham, Leicestershire
Tel: Empingham (078 086) 321 or (078 086) 770 (for bookings)

Location: Off A606, Whitwell, near Oakham

THE WATER:	3,100 acres. Lodge facilities. WCs. Changing rooms, showers, weighing-in room. Equipped with scales, measuring boards, gutting facilities and a deep freeze. Disabled anglers' facilities. Lounge, hot and cold drinks from vending machine. No limit to number of rods per day.
SEASON:	Early April to end October.
HOURS:	One hour before sunrise, or 4.30 a.m., whichever is later, to one hour after sunset.

COSTS:		Price band (£)
	Full rod (8 fish per day)	210.00–250.00
	Weekday rod	160.00–195.00
	Day ticket (8 fish)	5.50–7.00
	Evening ticket (after 5.00 p.m., 3 fish)	3.50–4.50

	Juveniles (12–15 years) half price. Second permit available, 16 fish maximum per day. Lodge opens at 5.30 a.m. for sale of permits and allocation of boats not previously booked.
BOATS:	Boats available from 8.30 a.m. for 2 or 3 anglers. Costs: Motor boat: £15.00–16.50 per day £9.00–10.50 per evening Rowing boat: £7.00–8.50 per day £4.00–5.00 per evening.
STOCKING POLICY:	Stock about 130,000 fish per year. Approximately 33% browns and 67% rainbows. Also a few thousand brooks.
PERMITS:	No reservations required. Anglian Water Authority Regional or Welland & Nene Water Authority licence required. Tickets may be obtained from above address or at Whitwell Lodge. (Tel: Empingham (078 086) 770.) Boat reservations recommended.
GENERAL INFORMATION:	Trolling permitted in designated areas. Juveniles over 12 years of age and under 16 must be accompanied by an adult (18 or over) who must accept full responsibility for juveniles. Children under 12 not permitted to fish.

ST. ALGARS FARM
West Woodlands, Frome, Somerset
Tel: Maiden Bradley (098 53) 233

Location: On B3092. 4 miles south of Frome

THE WATER:	2 acres. Maximum number of rods per day: 5–6.	
SEASON:	1 April to 31 October.	
HOURS:	According to time of year.	
COSTS:	Day ticket (4 fish)	*Price band (£)* 6.00–7.50
	No additional day tickets available.	
STOCKING POLICY:	Rainbows 1 lb to 3 lb.	
PERMITS:	Telephone reservations requested. Local authority licence required, not available at lake.	

SCALING RESERVOIR
Cleveland
c/o Tees Division, Trenchard Avenue, Thornaby, Stockton, Cleveland
Tel: Stockton (0642) 62216

Location: Close by the A171 — Guisborough to Whitby Road. Within North York Moors National Park

THE WATER:	105 acres. Altitude 607 ft. Lodge facilities. WC. No limit to number of rods per day.	
SEASON:	22 March to 31 October.	
HOURS:	6.00 a.m. to 6.30 p.m.	
		Price band (£)
COSTS:	Day ticket (8 fish, 9 in. minimum size)	4.20 +
	OAP, disabled, children under 16	2.10 +
STOCKING POLICY:	Rainbows.	
PERMITS:	No reservations required. Self service facilities for day tickets. Yorkshire Water Authority Licence required. For list of places where licences are sold, contact Yorkshire Water Authority, 21 Park Square South, Leeds, Yorkshire.	
GENERAL INFORMATION:	5,400 fish taken by 5,511 (recorded) rods. Worm or fly. Accommodation, caravan and camping sites nearby.	

SCOUT DIKE RESERVOIR
c/o Yorkshire Water Authority, West Riding House, Albion Street, Leeds
Tel: Leeds (0532) 448201

Location: Near Penistone, South Yorkshire; 15 miles from Sheffield; route via A61/A629

THE WATER:	38 acres. No lodge facilities. Chemical WCs situated around reservoir. No limit to number of rods.
SEASON:	25 March to 30 September.
HOURS:	7.00 a.m. to dusk.
COSTS:	Day ticket (2 fish, 12 in. minimum size) *Price band (£)* 1.50–2.25 No additional tickets available.
STOCKING POLICY:	Stocking with browns and rainbows before the commencement of season, then monthly throughout season.
PERMITS:	No reservations required. Day tickets sold by ticket-dispensing machines at the reservoir. No half-day tickets. Yorkshire Water Authority licence required by all anglers age 10 and over, not sold at reservoir.
GENERAL INFORMATION:	Fly, worm or spinning.

SELSET RESERVOIR
Co. Durham
c/o Northumbrian Water Authority, Tees Division, Trenchard Avenue, Thornaby, Stockton, Cleveland
Tel: Stockton (0642) 62216

Location: South of the B6276 Middleton-in-Teesdale to Borough road, about 5 miles from Middleton

THE WATER:	625 acres. Altitude 1,037 ft. Lodge facilities. WC. No limit to number of rods per day.	
SEASON:	1 April to 30 September.	
HOURS:	6.00 a.m. to 7.00 p.m.	
		Price band (£)
COSTS:	Day ticket (no bag limit, 9 in. minimum size)	2.00 +
	OAP, disabled, children under 16	1.00 +
PERMITS:	No reservations required. Self service facilities for day tickets. Northumbrian Water Authority licence required. Contact Tees Division (address above).	
GENERAL INFORMATION:	Fly only. Browns only. Unstocked. 470 fish taken by 347 (recorded) rods.	

SHELMORE TROUT FISHERY
Norbury, near Gnosall, Staffordshire
Tel: Woodseaves (078 574) 205

Location: Near A519/B5405

THE WATER:	Two lakes of 1 acre each. Cabin with log burner. Flies and food available. Maximum number of rods per day: 12.
SEASON:	Mid-March to 31 December.
HOURS:	March, April and May: 8.30 a.m. to dusk June, July, August: 7.30 a.m. to dusk September, October, November, December: 8.30 a.m. to dusk.
COSTS:	Day ticket (2 fish) *Price band (£)* 8.50–10.00
	Additional day tickets available, same price as above.
STOCKING POLICY:	Restocked daily. 150+ per acre. Minimum size 2 lb, up to 16 lb. Average weight: 3 lb.
PERMITS:	Reservations recommended. Severn Trent Water Authority licence required, not available on site.
GENERAL INFORMATION:	Employing a barbless hook, fish may be returned. Retention of the second fish terminates fishing for the day.

SHUSTOKE RESERVOIR
Shustoke, Coleshill, Warwickshire
c/o Tame House, Newhall Street, Birmingham
Tel: 021-233 1616

Location: Near Coleshill, about 10 miles from Birmingham

THE WATER:	100 acres.	
SEASON:	Mid-April to mid-October. First 3 days for season permit holders only.	
HOURS:	6.00 a.m. to one hour after sunset.	
COSTS:		*Price band (£)*
	Full rod (7 days a week, 4 fish)	95.00–120.00
	Full rod (weekdays only, 4 fish)	65.00–85.00
	Day ticket High Season (4 fish)	4.00–5.50
	Day ticket Low Season (4 fish)	3.60–5.50
	Concessionary day ticket (2 fish)	1.90–2.75
	Concessionary permits available for children under 16, disabled, OAP. Advance booking and permits from Tame House (address above).	
BOATS:	15 boats available. Costs: £1.90–2.75 per day up to 4.00 p.m. or per day after 4.00 p.m. Evening boats reduced rate.	
STOCKING POLICY:	2,500 browns, 3,500 rainbows.	
PERMITS:	10 day tickets available per day. Severn-Trent Water Authority licence required.	
GENERAL INFORMATION:	4,826 fish caught during season. No fly or lure exceeding 2 in. and bearing more than one single hook may be used.	

SIBLYBACK LAKE
St. Cleer, near Liskeard, Cornwall
Contact: South West Water Authority, 3–5 Barnfield Road, Exeter, Devon
Tel: Exeter (0392) 31666

Location: Off A390/B3254. Near Redgate and St. Cleer

THE WATER:	140 acres. Refreshments available at peak times. No limit to number of rods.	
SEASON:	1 April to 31 October.	
HOURS:	One hour before sunrise to one hour after sunset.	
COSTS:		Price band (£)
	Day ticket (5 fish)	4.50–6.00
	OAP, disabled, student under 18, junior under 16	3.50–5.00
	Child under 14	1.00–1.50
	Evening (after 4.00 p.m., 3 fish)	2.50–3.50
	Book of 20 permits available at 15% discount. No additional day tickets available.	
BOATS:	Pulling boats available, seats 2. Anchors provided. No boats Thursdays or Fridays. No boats after 12 October. Costs: £4.50–5.50 per day. £3.00–3.50 half day (after 4.00 p.m.). Telephone Liskeard (0579) 42366 to book.	
STOCKING POLICY:	Pre-season stocking of browns and rainbows, then trickle stocking throughout season with fish averaging over 1 lb.	
PERMITS:	No reservations required. Tickets on self-service, no change available. No local water authority licence required.	
GENERAL INFORMATION:	Brightly-coloured lures account for many fish early season. Late May normally sees fantastic hatches of Hawthorns followed by sedge hatches throughout the summer. Small flies invariably do best and particularly near the surface. September brings a feeding frenzy as Daddy Longlegs drift onto the water. 6,922 fish caught during season. 1.7 fish per rod day.	
	South West Water Authority.	

SIBSON FISHERIES
New Lane, Stibbington, Peterborough
Tel: Stamford (0780) 782621

Location: Off A1

THE WATER:	$2\frac{1}{2}$ acres. Maximum number of rods per day: 8.	
SEASON:	1 April to 31 October.	
HOURS:	Dawn to dusk.	
COSTS:		*Price band (£)*
	Day ticket (5 fish)	10.00–12.00
	Half-day ticket (2 fish)	6.00–7.50
	Additional tickets available, same price as above.	
STOCKING POLICY:	Stocking once per month if necessary. 75% rainbows, 25% browns.	
PERMITS:	Reservations required. Anglian Water Authority licence required, not available on premises.	
GENERAL INFORMATION:	Beginning of the season: dry fly. Middle to end of season: sinking line with fairly heavy lure. Fully furnished fishing cottage available (sleeps four).	

SOUTHEND FARM TROUT FISHERY
Southend Lane, Waltham Abbey, Essex
Tel: Lea Valley 715283/716480

Location: Turn left off the A104 from London at the Wake Arms roundabout in the direction of Waltham Abbey; turn right at the Woodbine pub into Woodgreen Road. About 500 yards down the road turn left into Southend Lane, drive to the end of the lane into the farm parking area

THE WATER:	4 acres. Shelter for eating and resting. Maximum number of rods per day: 25.	
SEASON:	Open all year.	
HOURS:	Daylight to dusk.	
COSTS:		*Price band (£)*
	Day ticket (3 fish)	9.00–10.50
	Half-day ticket (2 fish)	7.00–8.00
	Young people charged for actual fish caught; must be accompanied by an adult. Additional day tickets available.	
STOCKING POLICY:	Stocking daily. Rainbows only. 125 to the acre. Weight range: 1 lb to 10 lb.	
PERMITS:	Reservations advisable. Thames Water Authority licence required.	
GENERAL INFORMATION:	Most fishermen catch their limit. The lake is a uniform depth with the very deep area clearly marked.	

SPINNAKER LAKE
Baker's Farm Leisure Limited, Cerney Wick, Gloucestershire
Tel: Swindon (0793) 750016

Location: Off the A419, north of Swindon, on Spine Road

THE WATER:	55 acres.	
SEASON:	Opens mid-March.	
HOURS:	7.00 a.m. to one hour after sunset.	
		Price band (£)
COSTS:	Day ticket (6 fish)	6.00–7.00
	Evening ticket (from 5.00 p.m., 2 fish)	3.00–4.00
	No limit bag	10.00–11.50
	All prices include VAT.	

STAFFORD MOOR FISHERY
Dolton, Winkleigh, North Devon
Tel: Dolton (080 54) 360/371/363

Location: On the B3220 Exeter-Bideford road, midway between Winkleigh and Beaford

THE WATER:	14 acres. Lodge. WC. Large selection of flies available for sale.	
SEASON:	End March to late October.	
HOURS:	9.00 a.m. to one hour after sunset.	
		Price band (£)
COSTS:	Day ticket (4 fish)	7.50–9.50
	Evening ticket (2 fish)	4.50–6.50
	Additional day tickets available.	
STOCKING POLICY:	Stocked as required from fish cage anchored in lake. Fish average 2 lb.	
PERMITS:	Reservations recommended. Water authority licence not required.	
GENERAL INFORMATION:	Average 2 fish per rod.	

STITHIANS RESERVOIR
Stithians, near Redruth, Cornwall
Tel: Truro (0872) 3541

Location: Off A394

THE WATER:	274 acres. No lodge facilities. No limit to number of rods.	
SEASON:	15 March to 12 October.	
HOURS:	One hour before sunrise to one hour after sunset.	
		Price band (£)
COSTS:	Full rod	20.00–25.00
	Children under 14	5.00–6.50
	OAP, disabled, student under 18, junior under 16 – half price	
	Day ticket	1.50–2.25
	No bag limit.	
STOCKING POLICY:	Natural browns, rainbows and brooks stocked as fry.	
PERMITS:	No reservations required. Day permits on self-service, change not available. No local water authority licence required.	
GENERAL INFORMATION:	Many shallow bays at this water offer excellent sport with wild fish. Traditional nymph and dry fly tactics work best.	
	South West Water Authority.	

STRATFIELD SAYE
Wellington Enterprises, Stratfield Saye, Reading, Berks
Tel: Basingstoke (0256) 882882

Location: Situated between Reading and Basingstoke off the A33, immediately adjacent to Broadford Bridge

THE WATER:	Two lakes of 5 acres and 9 acres. Lodge facilities available. Flies available. Maximum number of rods per day: 12.	
SEASON:	1 April to 15 October.	
HOURS:	8.30 a.m. to dusk.	
COSTS:		*Price band (£)*
	Full rod (1 named day per week, 4 fish)	225.00–260.00
	Half rod (1 named day per fortnight, 4 fish)	115.00–140.00
	Day ticket (4 fish)	10.00–12.00
	Evening ticket (2 fish)	6.00–7.50
	All prices include VAT	
	No additional day tickets available.	
STOCKING POLICY:	Weekly stocking. 70% rainbows, 20% browns and 10% brooks. Weight range: $1\frac{1}{4}$ lb to 10 lb.	
PERMITS:	Reservations required. Thames Water Authority licence required.	
GENERAL INFORMATION:	No lures or droppers. Only one fly or nymph on line, on size No. 8 hook or smaller, $\frac{3}{4}$ in. maximum. 2,863 fish taken by 1,000 rods. Flies: April: Black and Peacock, Pheasant Tail May & June: Mayflies dry, Dry Olives, Dry Red and Grey Wulfs, Mayfly Nymphs July, August: Amber Nymphs, Corixa, Damsel Fly Nymph.	

SUNDRIDGE TROUT LAKES
Sundridge, near Sevenoaks, Kent
Contact Fishery Manager: Peter Leith, 10 Whitefoot Lane, Bromley, Kent
Tel: 01-698 9088

Location: Junction of A21 and A25. Entrance is on A25 Westerham Road at Main Road Sundridge. Opposite Smarts Garden Centre

THE WATER:	Two lakes at 15 acres and 5 acres. Two huts for members' use. Car park adjacent to lake. Season only. 100 members maximum.	
SEASON:	1 April to 31 October.	
HOURS:	Dawn until dusk.	
COSTS:	Full rod (4 fish per day or 10 fish per week. Fish any or all 7 days until 10-fish limit is caught)	*Price band (£)* 150.00–175.00 + VAT (includes free use of boats)
	Young people (under 16 years of age) – half price.	
BOATS:	21 boats (16 single and 5 double). Private boats permitted. No reservations necessary. No charge.	
STOCKING POLICY:	Approximately 7,500 trout stocked per season. All sizes from 1 lb up. Record: rainbow 16 lb, brown 7½ lb. Stocking every 2 to 3 weeks of 500 rainbows. Browns resident in lakes.	
PERMITS:	Thames Water Authority licence required.	
GENERAL INFORMATION:	6,372 fish taken by 100 members. Lures in April fished off weir. Fishing very good off weir after rain. Wind has little effect. Scale down to small frys as naturals appear. The lakes fish fairly easily all season. Large lake: dry or wet line. Small lake: dry fly only.	

SUNNYDALE RESERVOIR
c/o Bingley Angling Club, 5 Highfield Road, Frizinghall, Bradford
No telephone

Location: ½ mile from East Morton, between Bingley and Keighley, West Yorkshire

THE WATER:	1 acre.	
SEASON:	25 March to 30 September.	
COSTS:	Day ticket (2 fish, 12 in. minimum size)	*Price band (£)* 1.00–1.50
	Club Membership required. Season tickets covering all club preserves available.	
STOCKING POLICY:	Stocked annually with rainbows, browns and American brooks. Also an indigenous stock of browns.	
PERMITS:	Day permits required in advance, obtainable from local tackle shops; The Pantry, in Morton village (open Sunday); or by post from club secretary. Yorkshire Water Authority licence required.	
GENERAL INFORMATION:	Club members have access to two smaller dams, two lengths of beck fishing, three lengths of the River Wharfe, four lengths of the River Aire.	

SUTTON BINGHAM
c/o Wessex Water Authority, P.O. Box 9, King Square, Bridgwater
Tel: (0278) 57333

Location: 4 miles south of Yeovil. Can be approached from A37 Dorchester road. Near Somerset/Dorset border

THE WATER:	142 acres. Lodge facilities. WC. No limit to number of rods per day.	
SEASON:	End March to 15 October.	
HOURS:	8.00 a.m. until one hour after sunset.	
COSTS:		Price band (£)
	Full rod	100.00–125.00
	Day ticket (6 fish)	4.50–6.00
	Day ticket with boat (6 fish)	7.50–9.00
	Evening ticket with boat (after 4.00 p.m.)	5.50–7.00
	Junior, OAP approximately half price. Full rod permits available from Divisional Fisheries and Recreations Officer, Somerset Division (address above).	
BOATS:	Single occupancy OK (except opening weekend). Anchors provided. Boats may be booked in advance.	
STOCKING POLICY:	Stocking every 8–14 days. Usually between 75 to 100 fish per acre. Size: between $1\frac{1}{4}$ lb and 2 lb. 75% rainbows, 25% browns.	
PERMITS:	No reservations required. Self-service kiosks for day tickets and boats. No water authority licence required.	
GENERAL INFORMATION:	30,000 fish stocked in total Wessex Water Authority reservoir area of 389 acres. 17,000 fish taken, between $1\frac{1}{2}$ lb and 4 lb.	

SWEETHOPE LOUGHS
Kirkharle, Newcastle upon Tyne, Northumberland
Tel: Kirkwhelpington (0830) 40249

Location: Near A68, near A696. Near Kirkwhelpington. Newcastle upon Tyne area

THE WATER:	Two lakes totalling 75 acres. Maximum number of rods per day: boats – 16, bank – 16.
SEASON:	Browns: late March to end September. Rainbows: 1 May to end November.
HOURS:	9.30 a.m. to 10.00 p.m. or earlier as days shorten.
COSTS:	Prices only available to individual enquirers.
BOATS:	Boats available, seats 2. No anchors provided. Reservations recommended.
STOCKING POLICY:	Annual stocking Upper Lake (browns) 1,000–1,500 Lower Lake (rainbows) 1,000
PERMITS:	Reservations advisable. Northumbrian Water Authority licence required, available in local tackle shops (not on premises).

SWINSTY RESERVOIR
c/o Yorkshire Water Authority, West Riding House, Albion Street, Leeds
Tel: Leeds (0532) 448201

Location: Washburn Valley. West of Harrogate, near A59, near Timble

THE WATER:	156 acres.	
SEASON:	25 March to 30 September.	
HOURS:	7.00 a.m. to dusk.	
COSTS:	Day ticket (4 fish, 10 in. minimum size)	*Price band (£)* 2.00–3.00
PERMITS:	No reservations required. Ticket dispensing machine at reservoir. Yorkshire Water Authority licence required by all anglers aged 10 and over.	
GENERAL INFORMATION:	Fly, worm, spinning or minnow.	

TENTERDEN TROUT WATERS
Coombe Farm, Tenterden, Kent
Tel: Tenterden (058 06) 3201

Location: Take A28 Ashford to Tenterden road, then St. Michael's to Shoreham Lane

THE WATER:	Three lakes totalling 5 acres. Lodge. Flies available.	
SEASON:	Beginning April to end October.	
HOURS:	9.00 a.m. to sunset.	
COSTS:	Day ticket (2 fish)	*Price band (£)* 9.00–10.50
PERMITS:	Reservations recommended.	
GENERAL INFORMATION:	Rod may continue to fish during the whole of the day, placing fish caught in a retainer basket, from which two may then be selected.	

THORNTON RESERVOIR
Thornton, Leicestershire
Tel: Bagworth (053 021) 7107
c/o Cambrian Fisheries, Afonwen, Nr. Mold, Clwyd.
Tel: Mold (0352) 82598

Location: West of Leicester, near M1/A50

THE WATER:	76 acres. WC.	
SEASON:	Beginning April to mid-October.	
HOURS:	8.00 a.m. to one hour after sunset.	
		Price band (£)
COSTS:	Full rod (6 fish per day)	100.00–125.00
	Day ticket (6 fish)	5.00–6.50
	Half day ticket	3.00–4.00
BOATS:	Rowing boats available from 8.00 a.m. Boats may be reserved. Cost: £4.00–4.50.	
STOCKING POLICY:	4,000 browns, 2,000 rainbows.	
PERMITS:	Severn-Trent Water Authority licence required.	
GENERAL INFORMATION:	4,969 fish caught during season. No fly or lure exceeding 2 in. in length and bearing more than one single hook may be used.	

THRUSCROSS RESERVOIR
c/o Yorkshire Water Authority, West Riding House, Albion Street, Leeds
Tel: Leeds (0532) 448201

Location: Washburn Valley, west of Harrogate

THE WATER:	142 acres.	
SEASON:	25 March to 30 September.	
HOURS:	7.00 a.m. to dusk.	
		Price band (£)
COSTS:	Day ticket (4 fish, 10 in. minimum size)	2.00–3.00
PERMITS:	No reservations required. Ticket dispensing machine at reservoir. Yorkshire Water Authority licence required by all anglers aged 10 and over.	
GENERAL INFORMATION:	Fly only.	

TINGRITH TROUT FARM
Tingrith, Milton Keynes, Bucks
Tel: Flitwick (052 57) 4012

Location: Near M1, between Junctions 12 and 13

THE WATER:	8 acres.	
SEASON:	Beginning April to beginning January.	
HOURS:	8.00 a.m. to dark.	
		Price band (£)
COSTS:	Day ticket	7.50–9.50
	Half day ticket	4.20–6.00

TITTESWORTH RESERVOIR
near Leek, Staffs.
Tel: 053 834 389
c/o STWA Office, Westport Road, Burslem, Stoke-on-Trent
Tel: 0782 85601

Location: Approximately 2 miles from Leek. Near A53

THE WATER:	109 acres. Lodge facilities. WC. Maximum number of rods per day: 80.
SEASON:	Mid-April to mid-October.
HOURS:	One hour before sunrise to half hour after sunset.

COSTS:		*Price band (£)*
	Full rod (6 fish per day)	95.00–120.00
	Day ticket High Season (6 fish)	4.00–5.50
	Day ticket Low Season (6 fish)	3.60–5.50
	Concessionary day ticket (3 fish)	1.90–2.75

	Concessionary permits available for children under 16, disabled, OAP. Advance booking, permits and information from Fishing Lodge, Tittesworth Reservoir. Season permits and day tickets available from STWA Office (address above).
BOATS:	Rowing boats available. Costs: 15 ft. rowing boat: £3.80–4.75, 12 ft. rowing boat: £3.20–4.50. After 6.00 p.m.: £2.50–3.00.
STOCKING POLICY:	7,500 browns, 7,000 rainbows and 1,000 American brooks.
PERMITS:	Severn-Trent Water Authority licence required.
GENERAL INFORMATION:	No fly or lure exceeding 2 in. in length and bearing more than one single hook may be used. 4,985 fish taken during season.

TOFT NEWTON RESERVOIR
Market Rasen, Lincolnshire
Tel: Normanby-by-Spital (06737) 453

Location: Near Market Rasen. Off A631, near A15, near A1103

THE WATER:	40 acres. Lodge facilities. WC. Tackle for sale or hire. Tuition courses available. Maximum number of rods per day: 60.
SEASON:	1 April to end October.
HOURS:	One hour before sunrise to one hour after sunset.

		Price band (£)
COSTS:	Day ticket (8 fish)	5.50–6.50
	Juvenile day ticket (age: 12–15, 8 fish)	2.75–3.50

Additional day tickets available.

STOCKING POLICY:	At least 50 fish per acre. Average 1.83 fish per return. Season stocking: 6,276 rainbows (average weight 1.47 lb); 6,975 browns (average weight 1.23 lb). Stocked weekly.
PERMITS:	Reservations advisable first week of season and Bank holiday weekends. Self-service facilities in lodge. Anglian Water Authority rod licence required, available from office only when part-time bailiff in attendance. Anglers advised to purchase licence beforehand if possible.

GENERAL INFORMATION:	5,618 permits issued, 5,147 returns made.
	5,365 rainbows and 4,032 browns caught.
	    Successful flies: April: Lures, black, white muddlers. May: Corixa, white dolls, green and brown nymphs. June: Small lures, nymphs. July: Dry sedge, nymphs sub-surface. August: Nymphs and evening dry olive, sedge. September: Stickleback imitations, deep sunk white and orange lures, surface stripped muddlers. October: Stickles, white lures, green dolls, orange and green nymphs.
	    The reservoir is wind-dominated and of the 'concrete-bowl with clay bottom' type. The concrete banks have a wavy-wall finish to permit safe angling but no wading allowed. Light tackle best on windward ripple, heavy shooting heads for lee shores.
	    Fish weed patches. Fish rippled water and watch for slightest line movement when nymphing. Use 4 lb minimum breaking strain leader.
	
	Anglian Water Authority

TRIMPLEY RESERVOIR
Trimpley, near Kidderminster, Hereford and Worcester
c/o Tame House, Newhall Street, Birmingham 3
Tel: 021-233 1616

Location: Trimpley near Kidderminster. Near B4190/A442

THE WATER:	29 acres.	
SEASON:	Mid-April to mid-October.	
HOURS:	6.00 a.m. to one hour after sunset.	
		Price band (£)
COSTS:	Full rod (weekdays only)	54.00–65.00
	Full rod (weekends only)	38.00–45.00
	Day ticket High Season	4.00–5.50
	Day ticket Low Season	3.60–5.50
	Concessionary ticket	1.90–2.75
	Bag limit: Weekdays 4 fish, Weekends 6 fish. Concessionary permits available for children under 16, disabled, OAP. Advance booking and permits from Tame House (address above).	
BOATS:	Two boats available. Costs: Day up to 4.00 p.m. or Day after 4.00 p.m.: £1.50–1.80. Evening boats reduced rate.	
STOCKING POLICY:	300 browns, 2,700 rainbows.	
PERMITS:	Severn-Trent Water Authority licence required.	
GENERAL INFORMATION:	2,601 fish caught during season.	

TUNSTALL RESERVOIR
Co. Durham
Tel: Wolsingham (095 65) 7293
c/o Northumbrian Water Authority, Wear Division, Wear House, Abbey Road, Pity Me, Durham
Tel: Durham (0385) 44222

Location: 3 miles north of Wolsingham in Weardale

THE WATER:	112 acres. Altitude 720 ft. Lodge facilities. WC. No limit to number of rods per day.	
SEASON:	1 April to 31 October.	
HOURS:	6.00 a.m. to 6.30 p.m.	
		Price band (£)
COSTS:	Full rod (8 fish, 9 in. minimum size)	100.00 +
	OAP, disabled and children under 16	50.00 +
	Day ticket (8 fish, 9 in. minimum size)	4.00 +
	OAP, disabled and children under 16	2.00 +
	Weekly ticket	16.00 +
	OAP, disabled and children under 16	8.00 +
BOATS:	Rowing boats available from 8.30 a.m., seats 2. May be reserved. Costs: £5.00+ per day £3.00+ per evening.	
STOCKING POLICY:	Rainbows only.	
PERMITS:	No reservations required. Self-service facilities for day tickets. Northumbrian Water Authority licence required. Contact Wear Division (address above).	
GENERAL INFORMATION:	Fly only. Accommodation, camping and caravan sites nearby. 5,044 fish taken by 3,275 (recorded) rods.	

ULLEY RESERVOIR
c/o Yorkshire Water Authority, West Riding House, Albion Street, Leeds
Tel: Leeds (0532) 448201

Location: East of Sheffield. 4 miles from Rotherham, South Yorkshire, route via A618

THE WATER:	30 acres. No lodge facilities. WCs available. No limit to number of rods.	
SEASON:	25 March to 30 September.	
HOURS:	7.00 a.m. to dusk.	
		Price band (£)
COSTS:	Day ticket (2 fish, 11 in. minimum size)	1.50–2.25
	Half day ticket	.90–1.15
	Concessionary fishing tickets are available for juveniles aged up to and including 15 years. No additional day tickets available.	
STOCKING POLICY:	Stocking with browns and rainbows before the commencement of season, then monthly throughout season.	
PERMITS:	No reservations required. Day and half-day tickets sold by ticket dispensing machines at the reservoir. Yorkshire Water Authority licence required by all anglers age 10 and above, not sold at reservoir.	

UNDERBANK RESERVOIR
c/o Yorkshire Water Authority, West Riding House, Albion Street, Leeds
Tel: Leeds (0532) 448201

Location: Near Stocksbridge, 13 miles north-west of Sheffield, South Yorkshire. Route via A616

THE WATER:	103 acres. No lodge facilities. Chemical WCs situated around the reservoir. No limit to number of rods.	
SEASON:	25 March to 30 September.	
HOURS:	7.00 a.m. to dusk.	
COSTS:		*Price band (£)*
	Day ticket (2 fish, 11 in. minimum size)	1.50–2.25
	Half-day ticket	.90–1.15
	Concessionary fishing tickets are available for juveniles aged up to and including 15 years. No additional day tickets available.	
STOCKING POLICY:	Stocking with browns and rainbows before commencement of season, then monthly throughout the season.	
PERMITS:	No reservations required. Day and half-day tickets sold by ticket-dispensing machines at the reservoir. Yorkshire Water Authority licence required by all anglers aged 10 and above, not sold at reservoir.	

UPPER TAMAR LAKE
near Bude, Cornwall
Tel: Kilkhampton (028882) 262

Location: Near Kilkhampton, off A39, near B3254

THE WATER:	81 acres. Flies and limited tackle for sale. Sets of tackle for hire. Refreshments available at peak times. No limit to number of rods.
SEASON:	1 April to 31 October.
HOURS:	One hour before sunrise to one hour after sunset. Anglers fishing before 9.00 a.m. should use the lower car park at the entrance to Upper Tamar.

		Price band (£)
COSTS:	Day ticket (5 fish)	4.50–6.00
	OAP, disabled, student under 18, junior under 16	3.50–5.00
	Child under 14	1.00–1.50
	Evening (after 4.00 p.m., 3 fish)	2.50–3.50

Book of 20 permits available at 15% discount.
No additional day tickets available.

BOATS:	Pulling boats available, seats 2. Anchors provided. No boats on Thursdays. Costs: £4.50–5.50 per day. £3.00–3.50 half day (after 4.00 p.m.) Telephone Warden to book.
STOCKING POLICY:	Pre-season stocking of browns and rainbows, then trickle stocking throughout season with fish averaging over 1 lb.
PERMITS:	No reservations required. Tickets on self-service, no change available. No local water authority licence required.
GENERAL INFORMATION:	7,476 fish caught during season. 1.7 fish per rod day. Yellow or Black Lures do well early season, namely Viva and Yellow Matuka. Buzzers and Hawthorn hatches provide good surface sport from end of May, with sedge late in the summer. Daddy Longlegs supply excitement at the end of the season when floating artificials are eagerly taken when pre-occupation with buzzers allow. Particularly good flies are Green and Black Buzzers, Pheasant Tail Nymph, teal and green, Wickham's Fancy, Mallard and Claret, and, of course, Black and Peacock Spider.

South West Water Authority

VICARAGE SPINNEY LAKE
Little Linford, Newport Pagnell, Bucks
Tel: Newport Pagnell (0908) 62 6534

Location: Near M1, near A422. Near Newport Pagnell

THE WATER:	5 acres. Lodge, tackle, flies and food available. Maximum number of rods per day: 20.	
SEASON:	Mid-march to end October.	
HOURS:	8.00 a.m. to 9.00 p.m.	
		Price band (£)
COSTS:	Full rod (4 fish per day)	240.00–270.00
	Day ticket (4 fish)	9.20–10.25
	Additional day tickets available, same price as above.	
STOCKING POLICY:	100 per acre, weekly, as required. 50% $1\frac{1}{2}$ lb to 2 lb; 30% 2 lb to 5 lb; 20% 5 lb and upwards. Browns 30%, rainbows 70%.	
PERMITS:	Reservations required, only available from M. D. Sando, 6 Kipling Drive, Newport Pagnell, Bucks MK16 8EB. Tel: (0908) 62 6534. Anglian Water Authority rod licence (Gt. Ouse River Division) required, available on premises.	
GENERAL INFORMATION:	The lake is a flooded gravel pit with maximum depths of 20 feet – average depths of over 5 ft to within 10 ft of bank. The water is very rich in natural food and did support a healthy stock of coarse fish until its transformation to the trout fishery.	

WALL POOL LODGE
Gawsworth, Macclesfield, Cheshire
Tel: North Rode (026 03) 442

Location: 5 miles from Congleton. 3 miles from Macclesfield. On A536

THE WATER:	2 acres. Light snacks available to order. Maximum number of rods per day: 12.	
SEASON:	1 April to 30 November	
HOURS:	8.00 a.m. to dusk.	
		Price band (£)
COSTS:	Day ticket (8.00 a.m. to 4.30 p.m., 4 fish)	8.00–9.50
	Evening ticket (5.00 p.m. to dusk, 2 fish)	5.00–6.50
	Four hour session (2 fish)	5.00–6.50
	Additional day tickets are available once the first limit has been taken: £4.00–5.00.	
BOATS:	Two boats available, seats 2. Anchors provided. Reservations recommended.	
STOCKING POLICY:	Stocking daily. 200 fish per acre. Size: 1 lb to 8 lb. 75% rainbows, 25% American brooks and tigers.	
PERMITS:	Reservations advisable. No water board licence required.	

WALTHAMSTOW RESERVOIRS
Ferry Lane, Tottenham, London
Tel: 01-808 1527

Location: Near Waltham Forest, off A503, near A1006. Entrance near Underground and train stations

THE WATER:	Three reservoirs at 30 acres, 41 acres and 43 acres. WCs. Maximum number of rods per day: Brown trout water 120; rainbow trout water (fly only) 8 boat and 100 bank; rainbow trout water (any method) 100.
SEASON:	1 April to end October (brown trout water) 1 April to end November (rainbow trout water – fly only) 1 February to end November (rainbow trout – any method)
HOURS:	7.30 a.m. or sunrise (whichever is later) to thirty minutes after sunset.

		Price band (£)
COSTS:	Day ticket (6 fish)	6.00–7.00
	Part-day ticket	4.60–5.50

Book of 10 permits available at a discount of 10%.
Half price for under 16s except for first month of season when full price is charged.
Additional day tickets available, same price as above.

BOATS:	Four row boats available, seats 2 on rainbow (fly only) water. Costs: £4.00–4.50 per day. £3.00–3.50 part day.
STOCKING POLICY:	About 80 fish per acre on the rainbow trout (fly only) water; 70 fish per acre on any-method reservoir. 7,000 browns will be stocked. Twice weekly stocking. Aim to give average catch rate for the season of 1.5–2.0 fish per permit. Rainbows all over 12 in., browns all over 9 in., mostly over 12 in.
PERMITS:	Reservations advised for first week of season. Thames Water Authority licence required, available at reservoir.
GENERAL INFORMATION:	Thames Water Authority reservoir. 22,765 trout taken by 14,194 anglers. All three trout fishing reservoirs are used for water supply, and, apart from minor variations around culverts, the depth is a uniform 8 ft to 9 ft 4 in. The high throughput of water rich in nutrients, ensures an abundant supply of zooplankton from April to October. This provides the main source of food for the trout and the factors which determine its position are therefore of paramount importance.

Generally plankton is carried by wind generated currents to the downwind shore making this the most productive area. The brighter it is, the deeper the plankton will be so that in the absence of rising fish, try the downwind bank at a depth related to light intensity.

The inflows are always productive areas, especially during the warmer months.

WALTON HALL
Walton, The Balk, Wakefield, Yorkshire
Tel: Wakefield (0924) 257911

Location: Off A638/B6378

THE WATER:	40 acres.	
SEASON:	End March to end October.	
HOURS:	8.30 a.m. to sunset.	
		Price band (£)
COSTS:	Full rod	175.00–225.00
	Day ticket (midweek, 4 fish)	6.85–8.25
	Day ticket (weekend, 4 fish)	8.00–10.00
	Evening ticket (midweek, 2 fish)	4.65–5.75
	Evening ticket (weekend, 2 fish)	5.50–6.75
BOATS:	Boats available.	
GENERAL INFORMATION:	Meals available.	

WATTLEHURST TROUT LAKE
Wattlehurst Farm, Kingsfold, Horsham, Sussex
Tel: Oakwood Hill (030 679) 341

Location: On A24 — approximately 4 miles north of Horsham

THE WATER:	Approximately $1\frac{1}{2}$ acres. Maximum number of rods per day: 6.	
SEASON:	Beginning April to end October.	
HOURS:	8.00 a.m. to one hour after sunset.	
		Price band (£)
COSTS:	Day ticket (4 fish)	7.50–9.00
	Evening ticket (2 fish)	4.50–6.00
PERMITS:	Reservations required.	
GENERAL INFORMATION:	Largest hook size No. 10.	

WESTBURY FISHERY
Westbury Farm, Purley near Reading, Berks
Tel: Pangbourne 3123

Location: Off A329 near Purley, near Reading

THE WATER:	Three lakes of 3 acres, 4 acres and 9 acres. Rod room. Maximum number of rods per day: 10.	
SEASON:	1 April to 2 October.	
HOURS:	9.00 a.m. until half-hour after sunset.	
		Price band (£)
COSTS:	Full rod (1 day per week, 4 fish)	225.00–250.00
	Half rod (1 day per fortnight, 4 fish)	115.00–130.00
	Day ticket (4 fish)	12.50–14.00
	No additional day tickets available.	
STOCKING POLICY:	Stocked daily. Rainbows only. Size range: $1\frac{1}{2}$ lb to 8 lb.	
PERMITS:	Reservations required. No local water board licence required.	
GENERAL INFORMATION:	When the wind is in the north to east quarter, the fish are reluctant takers.	

WHALLEY ABBEY RESERVOIR
near Clitheroe, Lancashire
Bailiff – Tel: (025 482) 2151

Location: 4 miles south of Clitheroe on A59

THE WATER:	7 acres.	
SEASON:	Beginning April to end September.	
HOURS:	9.00 a.m. to one hour past sunset.	
		Price band (£)
COSTS:	Day ticket (4 fish)	£7.70–9.50
	Half-day ticket (3 fish)	5.80–8.00
	Tickets from: K. Varey, Tackle Shop, 4 New Market St, Clitheroe. Tel: Clitheroe (0200) 23267.	
PERMITS:	Reservations recommended.	

WHITESHEET FARM TROUT LAKES
Whitesheet Farm, Whitesheet, Wimborne, Dorset
Tel: Wimborne (0202) 884 504/883 687

*Location: Off the A31 Ringwood to Wimborne Road, at 'Old Thatched Inn'.
Right at crossroads from Wimborne, left on Colehill Road, to Whitesheet*

THE WATER:	Three lakes totalling approximately 7 acres. Maximum number of rods per day: 15.	
SEASON:	End March to mid-October	
HOURS:	8.00 a.m. to sunset.	
		Price band (£)
COSTS:	Day ticket	9.00–10.50
	Half day ticket	7.00–8.50
STOCKING POLICY:	About 100 fish per acre.	
PERMITS:	Reservations strongly recommended.	
GENERAL INFORMATION:	No lures. The lake is 30 ft at its deepest.	

WILLINGHURST TROUT FISHERY
Willinghurst Estate, Shamley Green, Surrey
Tel: Cranleigh (048 66) 71238

Location: Off B2128, near Cranleigh/Shamley Green

THE WATER:	Four lakes totalling 6 acres (largest 4 acres). Lodge. Facilities available for making hot drinks and cooking. Tackle and flies available on premises. Maximum number of rods per day: 12 (plus 2 evening rods).
SEASON:	1 April to mid-November.
HOURS:	9.00 a.m. until half an hour before dusk.
COSTS:	Day ticket (5 fish) — *Price band (£)* 11.50–13.00 No second ticket available.
STOCKING POLICY:	100–150 fish per acre. Twice per week. Approximately 250 fish per week. 1¼ lb to 10 lb. 80% rainbows, 20% browns.
PERMITS:	Reservations required. Thames Water Authority licence required, not available on premises.
GENERAL INFORMATION:	Average fish per rod: 2.9. About 50% of the fish caught are taken on lures, fishing slowly close to the bottom. About 40% of fish caught are taken by a nymph, fished close to surface, or, alternatively, on a long leader some feet below surface.

WIMBLEBALL LAKE
Brompton Regis, near Dulverton, Somerset
Tel: Brompton Regis (039 87) 372

Location: Near B3190, near Brompton Regis

THE WATER:	374 acres. Flies and limited tackle for sale. Sets of tackle for hire. Refeshments available at peak times. No limit to number of rods.
SEASON:	1 May to 31 October.
HOURS:	One hour before sunrise to one hour after sunset.

COSTS:		Price band (£)
	Day ticket (5 fish)	4.50–6.00
	OAP, disabled, full-time student under 18, junior under 16	3.50–4.50
	Child under 14	1.00–1.50
	Evening ticket (after 4.00 p.m., 3 fish)	2.50–3.50

Books of 20 permits available at 15% discount. No additional day tickets available.

BOATS:	Pulling boats available, seats 2. Costs: £4.50–5.50 per day. £3.00–3.50 half day (4.00 p.m.). Anchors provided. Telephone Warden to book. No boats after 12 October.
STOCKING POLICY:	Pre-season stocking of browns and rainbows, then trickle stocking throughout season with fish averaging over 1 lb.
PERMITS:	Reservations not required. Tickets on self-service, no change available. Local Water Authority licence not required.
GENERAL INFORMATION:	18,123 fish caught during season. 2.3 fish per rod day. In early season black flies and lures prove successful like Black and Peacock Spider, Black Gnat and Viva. Early morning fishing is exceptional as June comes, with fish close to the bank and often willing to rise to dry flies like sedge, Iron Blue Dun and Black Gnat. During the day fish tend to move to deeper water when teams of small wet flies (Mallard and Claret, Silver Invicta, Coachman) fished on the drift prove more successful than lures. By mid-summer small flies really show their worth, as the sedge hatch improves blow lining with a bushy sedge bringing exciting sport.

South West Water Authority

WISTLANDPOUND RESERVOIR
Blackmore Gate, near Barnstaple, Devon
Tel: South Molton (076 95) 2429

Location: Near A39, near B3226/B3358

THE WATER:	41 acres. No lodge facilities. No limit to rods.	
SEASON:	1 April to 31 October.	
HOURS:	One hour before sunrise to one hour after sunset.	

		Price band (£)
COSTS:	Day ticket (5 fish)	4.50–6.00
	OAP, disabled, student under 18, junior under 16	3.50–5.00
	Child under 14	1.00–1.50
	Evening (after 4.00 p.m., 3 fish)	2.50–3.50

Book of 20 permits available at 15% discount.
  No additional day tickets available.

STOCKING POLICY: Pre-season stocking of browns and rainbows, then trickle stocking throughout season with fish averaging over 1 lb.

PERMITS: No reservations required. Tickets on self-service, no change available. No local water authority licence required.

GENERAL INFORMATION: 4,147 fish caught during season. 1.7 fish per rod day. Black lures kill fish early season. Come May, teams of very small flies result in good catches, particularly Black and Peacock Spider, Black Buzzer, Pheasant Tail Nymph and assorted yellow patterns. These patterns continue their success through the season with Invicta from August and Daddy Longlegs in September.

South West Water Authority

WROUGHTON RESERVOIR
Overtown Hill Wroughton, Swindon, Wiltshire
Tel: Swindon (0793) 24331

Location: Near Swindon. Off A361/B4005. Near Junction 15, M4

THE WATER:	3 acres. Shelter. Maximum number of rods per day: 8.	
SEASON:	1 April to 30 November.	
HOURS:	8.00 a.m. to one hour after sunset.	
		Price band (£)
COSTS:	Day ticket (weekdays, 6 fish)	4.80–5.50
	Day ticket (Sundays/Bank Holidays, 6 fish)	5.50–6.25
	Part-day ticket (weekdays, 4 fish)	3.60–4.25
	Part-day ticket (Sundays/Bank Holidays, 4 fish)	4.10–5.00
BOATS:	Two punts available, seats 2. Costs: 55p–80p per punt.	
STOCKING POLICY:	Rainbows and browns stocked throughout the season.	
PERMITS:	Reservations advisable first week of season. Thames Water Authority licence required.	
GENERAL INFORMATION:	1.7 fish per rod average. No fishing on Saturday. Permits issued from the office: Cotswold Division, 17 Bath Road, Swindon SN1 4AT. Permits obtainable in advance by post. Advisable to telephone regarding availability of permits.	

Thames Water Authority

THE WATER AUTHORITIES

ANGLIAN WATER AUTHORITY
Diploma House, Grammar School Walk, Huntington PE18 6NZ
Tel: Huntington (0480) 56181

NORTHUMBRIAN WATER AUTHORITY
Northumbria House, Regent Centre, Gosforth, Newcastle-upon-Tyne
NE3 3PX
Tel: Gosforth (0632) 843151

NORTH WEST WATER AUTHORITY
Dawson House, Great Sankey, Warrington WA5 3LW
Tel: Penketh (092 572) 4321

SEVERN-TRENT WATER AUTHORITY
Abelson House, 2297 Coventry Road, Sheldon, Birmingham B26 3PU
Tel: Birmingham (021) 743 4222

SOUTHERN WATER AUTHORITY
Guildbourne House, Worthing, Sussex BN11 1LD
Tel: Worthing (0903) 205252

SOUTH WEST WATER AUTHORITY
3–5 Barnfield Road, Exeter EX1 1RE
Tel: Exeter (0392) 50861/31666

THAMES WATER AUTHORITY
New River Head, Rosebery Avenue, London EC1R 4TP
Tel: 01-837 3300

WESSEX WATER AUTHORITY
Techno House, Redcliffe Way, Bristol BS1 6NY
Tel: Bristol (0272) 25491

YORKSHIRE WATER AUTHORITY
West Riding House, 67 Albion Street, Leeds LS1 5AA
Tel: Leeds (0532) 448 201

THE LAKES LISTED BY COUNTY

AVON
Barrows Reservoirs
Blagdon Lake
Cameley Lakes
Chew Valley Lake

BEDFORDSHIRE
Little Heath Farm

BERKSHIRE
Stratfield Saye Lakes
Westbury Fishery

BUCKINGHAMSHIRE
Church Hill Farm
Latimer Park Lakes
Linford Lakes
Tingrith Trout Farm
Vicarage Spinney Lake

CAMBRIDGESHIRE
Block Fen Drove
Grafham Water
Sibson Fisheries

CHESHIRE
Wall Pool Lodge

CLEVELAND
Lockwood Beck Reservoir
Scaling Reservoir

CORNWALL
Argal Reservoir
Porth Reservoir
Siblyback Lake
Stithians Reservoir
Upper Tamar Lake

CUMBRIA
Coniston Water
Lake Windermere
Overwater Lake

DERBYSHIRE
Foremark Reservoir
Higham Farm Trout Fishery
Ladybower Reservoir
Linacre Reservoir
Ogston Reservoir

DEVON
Bellbrook Valley Trout Fishery
Burrator Reservoir
East Batsworthy Fishery
Fernworthy Reservoir
Kennick and Tottiford Reservoir
Stafford Moor Fishery
Wistlandpound Reservoir

DORSET
Flowers Farm Trout Lakes
Kingsbridge Lakes
Martins Trout Lake
Whitesheet Farm Trout Lakes

CO. DURHAM
Balderhead Reservoir
Blackton Reservoir
Burnhope Reservoir
Cow Green Reservoir
Derwent Reservoir
Grassholme Reservoir
Hury Reservoir
Selset Reservoir
Tunstall Reservoir

ESSEX
Ardleigh Reservoir
Chesterford Trout Fisheries
East Hanningfield Hall
Fishers Green
Hanningfield Water
Southend Farm Trout Fishery

GLOUCESTERSHIRE
Horseshoe Lakes
Spinnaker Lake

HAMPSHIRE
Allens Farm
Avington Trout Fishery
Bagwell Green
Bickton Mill Lakes
Bridge Farm Trout Lakes
Bull Meadow Lake
Damerham Fisheries
Hucklesbrook Trout Lakes
John O'Gaunts
Ladywell Lakes Trout Fishery
Leominstead Trout Fishery
Rooksbury Mill Trout Fishery

HEREFORD and
WORCESTERSHIRE
Trimpley Reservoir

HERTFORDSHIRE
Crown Netherhall Trout Fishery
Croxley Hall Waters
King's Langley Trout Fishery
Oughton Trout Fishery

HUMBERSIDE
Bridlington Trout Fishery

KENT
Bayham Lake Trout Fishery
Bewl Bridge Reservoir
Pooh Corner
Sundridge Trout Lakes
Tenterden Trout Waters

LANCASHIRE
Bank House Fly Fishery
Whalley Abbey Reservoir

LEICESTERSHIRE
Eye Brook Reservoir
Mill Farm Fishery
Rutland Water
Thornton Reservoir

LINCOLNSHIRE
Buckminster Park Lake
Hill View Trout Lake
Toft Newton Reservoir

LONDON
Barn Elms Reservoirs
Walthamstow Reservoirs

MIDDLESEX
Ashmere Fisheries
Kempton Park Reservoir

NORFOLK
Burebank Trout Fishery
Edgefield Hall Farm

NORTHAMPTONSHIRE
Elinor Trout Fisheries
Pitsford Reservoir
Ravensthorpe Reservoir
Ringstead Grange Trout Fishery

NORTHUMBERLAND
Bakethin Reservoir
Fontburn Reservoir
Kielder Water
Sweethope Loughs

NOTTINGHAMSHIRE
Colwick Park Reservoir
Cromwell Trout Lake

OXFORDSHIRE
Bushey Leaze
Farmoor Reservoir
Linch Hill: Stoneacres
Linch Hill: Willow Pool
Lockinge Fishery

SHROPSHIRE
Calvington Reservoir
Peatswood Lakes

SOMERSET
Clatworthy Reservoir
Durleigh Reservoir
Exe Valley Fishery
Hawkridge Reservoir
Otterhead Reservoir
St. Algars Farm
Sutton Bingham Reservoir
Wimbleball Lake

STAFFORDSHIRE
Gailey Trout Fishery
Patshull Park Fishery

Shelmore Trout Fishery
Tittesworth Reservoir

SUFFOLK
R.O.K. Pool Trout Fishery

SURREY
Frensham Trout Lake
Rushmoor Trout Lakes
Willinghurst Trout Fishery

SUSSEX
Ardingly Reservoir
Darwell Reservoir
Lakedown Trout Fishery
Newells Lake Fisheries
Peckham's Copse
Powdermill Reservoir
Wattlehurst Trout Lake

WARWICKSHIRE
Draycote Water
Shustoke Reservoir

WEST MIDLANDS
Packington Fisheries

WILTSHIRE
Broadfield Trout Lake
Lower Moor Fishery
Wroughton Reservoir

YORKSHIRE
Cod Beck Reservoir
Damflask Reservoir
Deer Springs
Elvington Lake
Farmire
Fewston Reservoir
Greenfield Lake
Leighton Reservoir
Malham Tarn Field Centre
Morehall Reservoir
Scout Dike Reservoir
Sunnydale Reservoir
Swinsty Reservoir
Thruscross Reservoir
Ulley Reservoir
Underbank Reservoir
Walton Hall

CONVERSION TABLES

WEIGHT

oz	oz or g	g	lb	lb or kg	kg
0.04	1	28.35	2.20	1	0.45
0.07	2	56.70	4.41	2	0.91
0.11	3	85.05	6.61	3	1.36
0.14	4	113.40	8.82	4	1.81
0.18	5	141.75	11.02	5	2.27
0.21	6	170.10	13.23	6	2.72
0.25	7	198.45	15.43	7	3.18
0.28	8	226.80	17.64	8	3.63
0.32	9	255.15	19.84	9	4.08
0.35	10	283.50	22.05	10	4.54
0.39	11	311.85	24.25	11	4.99
0.42	12	340.19	26.46	12	5.44
0.46	13	368.54	28.66	13	5.90
0.49	14	396.89	30.87	14	6.35
0.53	15	425.24	33.07	15	6.80
0.56	16	453.59	35.27	16	7.26
			37.48	17	7.71
			39.68	18	8.17
			41.89	19	8.62
			44.09	20	9.07

LENGTH

in	in or cm	cm	in	in or cm	cm
0.39	1	2.54	6.30	16	40.64
0.79	2	5.08	6.69	17	43.18
1.18	3	7.62	7.09	18	45.72
1.58	4	10.16	7.48	19	48.26
1.97	5	12.70	7.87	20	50.80
2.36	6	15.24	8.27	21	53.34
2.76	7	17.78	8.66	22	55.88
3.15	8	20.32	9.06	23	58.42
3.54	9	22.86	9.45	24	60.96
3.94	10	25.40	9.84	25	63.50
4.33	11	27.94	10.24	26	66.04
4.72	12	30.48	10.63	27	68.58
5.12	13	33.02	11.02	28	71.12
5.51	14	35.56	11.42	29	73.66
5.91	15	38.10	11.81	30	76.20